NEW VANGUARD 328

WARSHIPS IN THE WAR OF THE PACIFIC 1879–83

South America's ironclad naval campaign

ANGUS KONSTAM   ILLUSTRATED BY PAUL WRIGHT

OSPREY PUBLISHING

Bloomsbury Publishing Plc

Kemp House, Chawley Park, Cumnor Hill, Oxford OX2 9PH, UK

29 Earlsfort Terrace, Dublin 2, Ireland

1385 Broadway, 5th Floor, New York, NY 10018, USA

E-mail: info@ospreypublishing.com

www.ospreypublishing.com

OSPREY is a trademark of Osprey Publishing Ltd

First published in Great Britain in 2024

A catalogue record for this book is available from the British Library.

ISBN: PB 9781472861245; eBook 9781472861238; ePDF 9781472861221;
XML 9781472861214

24 25 26 27 28 10 9 8 7 6 5 4 3 2 1

Index by Fionbar Lyons
Typeset by PDQ Digital Media Solutions, Bungay, UK
Printed and bound in India by Replika Press Private Ltd.

Osprey Publishing supports the Woodland Trust, the UK's leading woodland
conservation charity.

To find out more about our authors and books visit
www.ospreypublishing.com. Here you will find extracts, author
interviews, details of forthcoming events and the option to sign up for our
newsletter.

All photos courtesy of Stratford Archive

CONTENTS

WARSHIPS IN THE WAR OF THE PACIFIC 1879–83

South America's ironclad naval campaign

INTRODUCTION

The War of the Pacific (also known as The Saltpeter War) of 1879–83 never really dominated the history books. In the naval world though, it was an important clash that proved the effectiveness of all those new technologies of the time; steam power, modern rifled guns and above all the supremacy of the ironclad. It was a war that went largely unnoticed outside South America, but which had major consequences for the future of the continent. When war came between Chile, Bolivia and Peru it was inevitable that the bulk of the fighting would take place at sea. Bolivia had no navy to speak of, while the other two countries lacked a land border but had long Pacific coastlines which were vulnerable to seaborne attack. So, victory would go to the country which could control the sea. This struggle for regional sea power would become a clash between two very different navies, and a test bed for the emerging naval technologies of the industrial age.

The Chilean Navy was larger and more modern than the Peruvian one, and so its strategy was to impose a blockade of the Peruvian coast. Its aim was to break Peru's fragile economy. Peru, though, had a trump card in the *Huascár*, a small but powerful British-built ironclad. Both navies would scramble to add other ironclads to their fleets, and the naval war would be dominated by these powerful modern warships and by the equally modern combination of rifled naval guns and reliable steam-powered warships. It was, arguably, the first truly modern naval war.

The conflict began as a territorial clash between Chile and Bolivia, but the

Today, the turret ship *Huascár* is an historic vessel, preserved for posterity in the Chilean port of Talcahuano. She acts as a floating museum, recounting the part she played in the War of the Pacific. *Huascár* is now the world's second-oldest surviving ironclad – the oldest being HMS *Warrior*.

latter then invoked its secret defensive alliance with Peru, and so the war spread. Bolivia then took a back seat as it lacked a fleet. The naval struggle between Chile and Peru which followed involved attempts to blockade the enemy coast, launch amphibious raids and bring the enemy into battle, the engagements fought between steam-powered and often ironclad warships. From a naval perspective, this was a fascinating war, fought not by the great powers of the Victorian era but by two newly emergent South American countries. It also involved more clashes between ironclads than the American Civil War, fought two decades before. This book explores the naval side of this little-known but historically crucial campaign, a naval struggle for sea power that helped reshape a continent.

The Pacific Coastlines of Bolivia, Chile and Peru

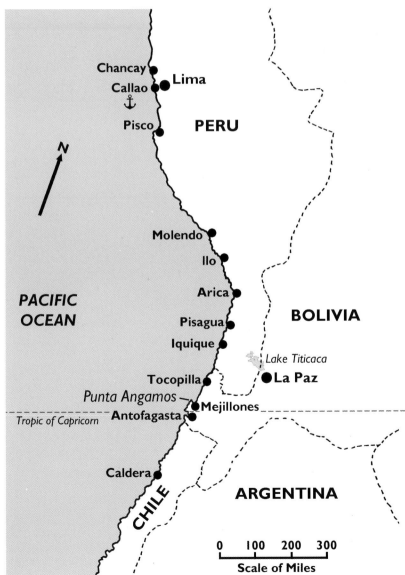

Elements of the Peruvian fleet at sea. The ironclad turret ship *Huascár* is shown in the centre, with the steam corvette *Unión* on the left and the steam gunboat *Pilcomayo* on the right. All three warships played major roles in the campaign.

The Bolivian port of Antofagasta was a centre for mining operations in the hinterland, dominated by the Atacama desert. Its capture by the Chileans in February 1879 marked the start of the war. The frontier-like port subsequently served as an advance base for the Chilean Navy.

BACKGROUND

The alternative name for the conflict, the Saltpeter war, reflects the *casus belli* for the conflict. During the mid-19th century clashes between the newly independent nations of South America were commonplace as the states vied for control of the continent's abundant natural resources. Several of these were over guano, or bird droppings. As early as 1804, the geographer von Humboldt, while voyaging along South America's Pacific coast, noted the busy local trade in seabird guano. He took samples home with him and confirmed they contained minerals which could greatly enhance the fertility of agricultural soil. Soon, guano harvesting was big business, with hundreds of tons of guano being shipped to North America and Europe every year.

So, bird droppings became an important commodity. The coasts of Bolivia, Peru and Chile contained the world's richest deposits of a mineral which the rest of the world needed for economic, agricultural and military development. In 1864, this even sparked a clash over ownership of the guano-rich Chincha Islands off the Peruvian coast, home to over 60 million seabirds. Guano deposits over 200ft high on the islands were the prize. Spain also demanded that Peru repay debts incurred during their war of independence. When the Peruvians refused, the Spanish seized the archipelago. Chile and Peru then formed an alliance and ejected the Spaniards, but the two neighbours, as well as Bolivia, then continued to clash over their control of guano and other minerals.

By 1870 though, the year when guano shipments were at their peak, it was clear that supplies were running out. This was particularly serious for Peru, as guano was the country's main export. The Peruvians responded by nationalizing the industry, but they were unable to avoid the growing shortage of guano. So, other sources of natural resources were sought. The most significant of these was sodium nitrate, also known as Chilean saltpeter. Like guano, it was primarily a fertilizer, but it was also used in the production of gunpowder and explosives. The largest accumulations of the mineral were found in the inhospitable Atacama desert, which bordered the Pacific and lay between Chile and Peru. This region, though, was actually owned by Bolivia. However, the Bolivian Pacific littoral had loosely defined borders, and as the mining of Chilean saltpeter became more lucrative, Chile began challenging Bolivia's ownership of this mineral-rich territory.

In 1866, the boundary between Bolivian and Chilean territory was established along the latitude of

24° South, just south of the Bolivian port of Antofagasta. A band of 70 miles on either side was dubbed a 'Mutual Benefits Zone', where the two countries would benefit from the taxation of mineral mining. This though, proved difficult to administer, particularly as many of the mineral companies operating in the Atacama desert were

The economy of the region was fuelled by the mining of nitrates – the collection of guano from the coast and the extraction of Chilean saltpeter from the arid Atacama desert. This image shows a mound of guano being excavated, formed from a century's-worth of seabird droppings.

Chilean. This was set against a growing atmosphere of distrust between Chile and its neighbours, brought on by a combination of border disputes and a marked rise in Chilean militarism. This led to Bolivia and Peru signing a secret pact of mutual defence in February 1873. It was hoped Argentina would join the alliance, but this never happened.

Still, a new Bolivian–Chilean treaty was negotiated in 1874, which allowed Bolivia to collect all tax revenues from mineral mining north of the 24° South border. In return, Chilean mining companies won a 25-year freeze of tax increases in the region to the north of the line. These included the *Compañía de Salitres y Ferrocarril de Antofagasta* (CSFA, or Antofagasta Nitrate and Railway Company), which had signed a major mining treaty with Bolivia's unstable President Melgarejo a few years before. Following Melgarejo's overthrow in 1871 though, the new Bolivian government renegotiated all of its mineral contracts, and in 1878 it demanded payment of a new tax of 10 cents per quintal (or hundredweight) of extracted minerals.

By then the CSFA had invested heavily in the region and had even built a single-track railway stretching 150km to the north-east, through the heart of the Atacama desert. The company refused the tax demand, as it broke the terms of the 1874 treaty. As a result, the new Bolivian government of President Daza confiscated the CSFA's property in the region. The company's Chilean and British directors then demanded that the Chilean government intervene on their behalf. The reason the Chilean president Anibal Pinto did so with military force is still the subject of historical debate, but the consensus is that Chile, like its neighbours, was suffering from a major economic crisis fuelled by the rapid decline in the guano trade. So, companies like the CSFA held considerable influence with Pinto's government. The outcome was that the two countries would go to war.

On 11 February 1879, a party of Chilean marines landed at the Bolivian littoral port of Antofogasta, to protect the CSFA's holdings there. Both sides mobilised their forces, while President Daza called on President Prado of Peru to honour his country's secret treaty. Then on 14 March, after President Pinto refused to withdraw from Antofagasta, Bolivia declared war on Chile. Three weeks later, on 6 April, Peru entered the war on Bolivia's side. The wholly needless War of the Pacific had begun. The conflict might have been unnecessary, and it was one which the protagonists were ill prepared for, but the stakes were high. By necessity the land battleground would be the arid Atacama desert, which was singularly unsuited to military operations, unless troops could be supplied from the coast. The real prize then, was not the seizure of territory but the control of the sea.

CHRONOLOGY

1879

11 February   Chilean forces occupy Bolivian Pacific port of Antofagasta.

14 March   Bolivia declares war on Chile.

4 April   Peru declares war on Chile.

21 May   Battle of Iquique (Peruvian victory). Naval clash at Punta Gruesa.

8 October   Battle of Angamos (Chilean victory), *Huascár* captured.

November   Peruvian warship *Pilcomayo* captured.

7 December   Blockade of Peruvian port of Arica begun.

24 December   Peruvian torpedo boat *Alay* captured in Ecuadorian port of Ballenita.

1880

27 February   Bombardment of Peruvian defences at Arica.

10 April   Blockade of Peruvian port of Callao begun.

26 May   Battle of Tacna (Bolivian–Peruvian army defeated), Bolivians knocked out of the war.

7 June   *Arica* captured by the Chileans.

July   Chilean warship *Loa* sunk by hidden explosive charge.

August   Chilean warship *Covadonga* sunk by hidden explosive charge.

November   Chilean amphibious operations conducted during advance on Lima.

The Chilean gunboat *Magallanes* carried a main armament of Armstrong RMLs, a 64-pdr (6⅜in) gun forward and this 115-pdr (7in) gun aft. Both were mounted on the centreline on a pivoting carriage while deck tracers allowed the guns to be deployed on either beam.

1881

17 January   Peruvian fleet at Callao scuttled. Callao captured by the Chileans.

1883

20 October   Treaty of Ancón signed between Chile and Peru. Tarapacá province ceded to Chile.

November   Chilean torpedo boat *Colo Colo* operates on Lake Titicaca.

1884

4 April   Treaty of Valparaiso signed between Chile and Bolivia. Bolivian Pacific littoral ceded to Chile.

THE NAVAL CAMPAIGN

The course of the campaign that followed was dictated by a combination of naval strength and geography. Bolivia had no navy, and the attempt by President Daza to licence privateers was strongly discouraged by Britain, France and the United States, who refused to recognize their legitimacy. So, the privateering notion was abandoned and the naval struggle would be fought between the small fleets of Chile and Peru. The Chilean Navy was larger, but the Peruvian included a handful of ironclads, so the struggle between the two fleets would be far from one-sided. However, in the naval campaign that followed, the geography of the Pacific coast would dictate its course and pace every bit as much as the capabilities of the rival warships.

Opening shots

From the start, the Chileans were keen to impose a naval blockade on the Chilean ports, which would allow them to land troops wherever they wished along the Bolivian and Peruvian Pacific coasts. For them, the amphibious landing at Antofagasta in February had shown just how effective this stratagem could be. On 5 April, the day after Chile and Peru officially

The Chilean fleet blockading the Peruvian port of Iquique in early 1879. The harbour beyond is filled with merchant ships, as the port was key to Peru's saltpeter trade. In the foreground are the two Chilean ironclads *Almirante Cochrane* and *Blanco Encalada*.

declared war, a Chilean squadron led by *Contralmirante* (Rear Admiral) Juan Williams Rebolledo steamed north to blockade the port of Iquique. His flagship *Almirante Cochrane* was accompanied by her sister ship *Blanco Encalada* and the steam corvettes *Chacabuco* and *Esmeralda*. President Pinto and his war cabinet had urged Williams to attack Peru's main naval base at Callao, but he sensibly decided it was too well protected.

Iquique, 640 miles to the south, was not only almost three days' steaming closer, but it was the centre of Peru's nitrate trade. The tax generated from Iquique amounted to almost three-quarters of Peru's national income. By blockading the port, used by over a thousand cargo ships a year, Chile could cripple Peru's economy at a single stroke. That, Williams argued, would force the Peruvians to come south to give battle – with a fight which could then be fought on terms which were favourable to the Chileans. The first naval clash of the war though didn't involve Williams' command at all.

At 10.30am on 12 April the Chilean steam gunboat *Magallanes* was heading north from Antofagasta, carrying orders for Williams, when she was ambushed by two Peruvian warships 65 miles south of Iquique. Word had reached the Peruvians that the unescorted Chilean transport *Copapó* was heading north to Iquique, and Capitán Garcia y Garcia was sent to intercept her with the corvette *Unión* and the gunboat *Pilcomayo*. He decided to lie in wait behind a headland just south of the Loa River, and that morning, when he spotted steam, Garcia was sure it was the transport. Instead, it was *Teniente* (Lieutenant) Lattore of the *Magallanes* who sprung the trap. When he spotted the waiting enemy he increased speed and headed towards Iqueque, with Garcia's two warships in hot pursuit. The *Unión* was slightly faster than the *Magallanes*, and so she gradually began overhauling her prey.

The ships exchanged fire, but Lattore's gunboat was only hit once, without suffering any real damage. At 12.55pm, a shot struck the *Unión* and her speed immediately began to drop. Garcia was forced to abandon the pursuit. Although the press dubbed this minor skirmish the 'Battle of Chipana', the name of a bay just north of the river, it was an inconclusive clash. After limping back to Callao, the *Unión* spent the rest of the month undergoing repairs to her steam pipes. It was also claimed that the ship lost 36 men dead and wounded. Still, both sides claimed a victory in this opening clash of the war.

Meanwhile, Williams was under increasing pressure to act more decisively. So, after less than two weeks of blockade he decided to head north to Callao to see what he could achieve there. By then he had been reinforced, and leaving the newly arrived corvette *Esmeralda* and the gunboat *Covadonga* to continue the blockade, he headed north, his fleet rendezvousing off

The small but powerful Chilean gunboat *Magallanes* was involved in the opening naval clash of the war on 12 April 1879, when she was ambushed and pursued by the Peruvian corvette *Unión* and the gunboat *Pilcomayo*. Skilful handling by her commander, Teniente Lattore, allowed the ship to evade her pursuers.

Pisagua, 36 miles to the north. He bombarded the small port on 18 April, after being fired on from the shore. He then withdrew out to sea and headed towards Callao, keeping well out of sight of the coast.

Williams' attacking fleet now consisted of the ironclads *Almirante Cochrane* and *Blanco Encalada*, the corvettes *O'Higgins*, *Chacabuco* and *Abtao*, the *Magallanes* and a collier. Williams' plan was simple. Laden with explosives, the *Abtao* would act as a fireship, and on reaching Callao she would enter the harbour and then be set ablaze. After pointing her towards the enemy, the crew would abandon ship. In the resulting confusion and under cover of a general bombardment, the Chilean warships would lower their steam launches, which had been specially fitted with spar torpedoes. These would then attack the Peruvian ironclads. However, when they arrived off Callao on 21 May the primary targets – the *Huascár* and the *Independencia* – were absent. An intercepted Italian merchantman reported that they had recently put to sea, escorting three small transports. Williams abandoned the assault and sped south to intercept the enemy squadron.

The battle of Iquique

He was too late. The two Peruvian ironclads as well as the transports had left Callao six days before, with President Prado embarked. On 20 May they reached Arica, where they learned that Williams had left Iquique, and only two ships remained on blockade. Prado went ashore, accompanied by the troops, while Capitán Don Miguel Grau of the *Huascár* led the two ironclads south to lift the Iquique blockade. Capitán Arturo Prat of the *Esmeralda* and Teniente Condell of the *Covadonga* had no inkling the Peruvians were at sea. Then, at 7.00am on 21 May, the *Huascár* was sighted heading towards them from the north. She was still five miles away, and Grau was followed by Capitán Moore of the *Independencia*, lagging two miles astern. Prat ordered Condell to pull back into shallower water closer to the harbour, where they waited for the enemy as their crews finished breakfast.

A

CHILEAN IRONCLADS *ALMIRANTE COCHRANE* (1) AND *BLANCO ENCALADA* (2)

In 1871 the Chilean government allocated funds for the building of two medium-sized ironclad warships. Having just emerged from a war with Spain, Chile was keen to protect her long coastline. They also wanted to create a fleet capable of holding its own in any future conflict, either with a European power or another South American one. Wisely, the Chileans hired the celebrated British naval architect Edward Reed to design these ships. Reed, a former Chief Constructor for the British Admiralty, was arguably the world's leading authority on ironclad warships, who had overseen the Royal Navy's move from broadside ironclads like HMS *Warrior* to central battery ones, where larger guns were carried, protected inside an armoured citadel. Although by then Reed was designing a new generation of oceangoing turret ships, he considered that the central battery design was better suited to Chile's needs, in terms of both cost and fighting potential. The result was the two-ship Almirante Cochrane class, completed in 1874–75. In the War of the Pacific these powerful and well-designed iron-hulled ironclads were mechanically reliable, considerably better-protected than their Peruvian counterparts, and their powerful battery of six Armstrong 9in guns virtually gave them an all-round arc of fire.

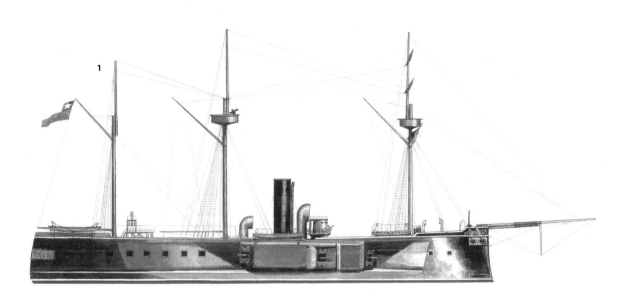

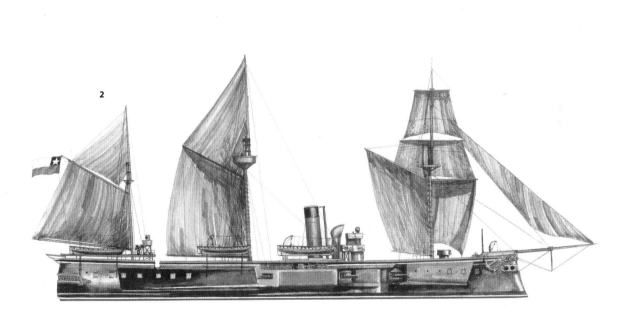

The final moments of the Chilean steam corvette *Esmeralda* during the battle of Iquique. After the sinking, the Peruvian ironclad *Huascár*, pictured on the right, moved in to rescue the survivors. Copy of an oil painting by Nicolá Guzmán Bustamente.

Grau approached cautiously, worried that the Chileans had deployed stationary torpedoes (mines) in his path. However, battle was finally joined at 8.00am, when *Huascár* opened fire with her powerful 10in guns. The struggle that followed is described in detail later – we only need to outline the basics here. That morning, *Huascár* engaged *Esmeralda*, leaving *Independencia* to take on *Covadonga*. On paper it should have been a very one-sided fight. That though, didn't take into account the courage and determination of Arturo Prat. Another key factor was the marked superiority of Chilean gunnery – the result of neglect in gunnery training by the Peruvians. Still, the *Esmeralda*'s shots bounced off *Huascár*'s armour. Then, as the range dropped rifle fire from embarked Chilean sharpshooters also had no effect whatsoever. Neither did the fire from Peruvian infantry and artillery who then joined in from the shore.

Huascár's opening shots had been fired at a range of over a mile, but this gradually reduced to about 800yds. Shortly after 10.15am, Prat headed further out to sea, presumably to avoid fire from the shore. The range then dropped rapidly, and even the abysmally inaccurate Peruvian gunners couldn't miss. At 10.30am, a shell exploded in *Esmeralda*'s boiler space, knocking out one boiler, damaging the other and killing several crewmen. With that, *Esmeralda*'s speed dropped to a walking pace. *Huascár* then attempted to ram her, but the bid failed and the two ships lay alongside each other. Seizing his moment, Prat and a marine sergeant leapt onto the Peruvian ironclad's deck, and tried to find a way inside her. However, after refusing to surrender, they were both cut down by small-arms fire.

Grau rammed the *Esmeralda* two more times, and the Chilean corvette finally sank at 1.30pm. The 63 survivors of her crew were taken prisoner. Meanwhile, the *Covadonga* steamed off to the south, pursued by the *Independencia*. Condell kept close inshore, but the range fell steadily and

When the *Huascár* and *Independencia* attacked the two Chilean ships blockading Iquique on 21 May 1879, the latter headed south in pursuit of the Chilean gunboat *Covadonga*. However, the *Independencia* ran aground on an uncharted rock off Punta Gruesa and was wrecked. In this copy of a painting by Thomas Somerscales, the *Covadonga* is shown firing at the ironclad, whose guns are unable to reply.

soon the ironclad was less than 150yds astern of her. At this angle, only one of the *Independencia*'s guns could bear on the gunboat, and she only scored one hit. *Covadonga*'s own stern guns hit the ironclad several times, but to no effect. Then, at 11.45am, fate intervened. Moore had planned to ram his opponent, as he had the faster ship. He ordered the ironclad's helm to be put over to starboard, so he could get a better ramming angle. Then a Chilean rifle bullet struck the ironclad's helmsman, whose wheel was outside the armoured citadel. Before a replacement helmsman could grab the wheel, the ironclad ran hard aground.

The *Covadonga* moved round to pepper the ironclad's defenceless stern, but was eventually driven off when the *Huascár* appeared. Moments before, the *Independencia* had raised a white flag, but this was quickly hauled down. The *Huascár* pursued the *Covadonga* for half an hour, and then returned to her stricken consort. It was now clear though that the *Independencia* was unsalvageable, so her crew were transferred to the *Huascár*, together with a pair of 150-pdr guns, and the wreck was abandoned. The unfortunate Moore was placed under arrest, pending a court martial. So, the battle of Iquique ended in what was essentially a Chilean victory. Both sides had lost a warship, but as an ironclad the *Independencia* was irreplaceable. Peruvian losses were just five dead and 18 wounded, compared with 149 killed on *Esmeralda* and 63 captured. The real victor, though, was Arturo Grau, who posthumously became a Chilean national hero. The more-successful Condell was all but forgotten.

Capitán Arturo Prat (1848–79) became a national hero in Chile during the war when his corvette *Esmeralda* was rammed by the Peruvian ironclad *Huascár*. Accompanied by a petty officer, Prat jumped aboard the enemy ship, but was shot before he could achieve anything.

The *Huascár*'s raids

For the next few months, Capitán Grau and the *Huascár* dominated the seas, from their base in Arica down to Antofagasta. *Huascár* even ventured south to cut the Chilean telegraph cable linking Valparaiso and Antofagasta. This in turn kept the Chilean army at bay, as advancing into the Bolivian Pacific littoral was impossible without supply from the sea. Damage from a shore-battery hit at Antofagasta led to urgent repairs, but the *Huascár* was back at sea again in early July. Meanwhile, Williams and the Chilean fleet resumed their blockade of Iquique. On the night of 9/10 July, the *Huascár* attacked the *Magallanes* off the port, but the Chilean gunboat put up a staunch fight. As Grau's gunnery was poor, he tried to ram his Chilean opponent twice, but failed both times. When the *Almirante Cochrane* appeared, the *Huascár* backed off and returned to Arica.

The Peruvian turret ship *Huascár*, pictured off the Morro at Arica. For much of 1879, the ironclad used the small Peruvian port as a base, while she and her wooden-hulled consort *Union* ranged along the coast, preying on Chilean shipping.

Then, on 17 July, *Huascár* and *Union* headed south to raid Chilean coastal transports which were attempting to land troops on the Bolivian coast. One of these, the *Rimac*, was captured with 300 troops still aboard. The national outcry this created in Chile led to Williams' replacement by the more aggressive Acting *Contralmirante interino* (Acting Commodore) Galvarino Riveros. He and Chile's new War Minister, Don Rafael Sotomayor, promptly changed their naval strategy. They abandoned the blockade of Iquique and

During the war, the Chileans bought 12 British-built torpedo boats from the Yarrow Shipyard at Poplar in East London. These arrived during the conflict, and some saw service during the blockade of Callao in 1880–81. These ones are pictured in Valparaiso after the war, by which point identifying numbers had been added to their funnels.

regrouped in the country's main naval base at Valparaiso. The ships underwent maintenance and bottom-cleaning by divers to improve their performance.

Meanwhile, the *Huascár* continued her raids south from Arica. In late August, she attempted a spectacularly unsuccessful torpedo attack on the *Abtao* as she lay anchored off Antofagasta. The torpedo turned in a circle and almost hit the *Huascár*. Only the quick thinking of a Peruvian officer, who dived into the water to fend it off, averted a self-inflicted disaster. Grau's raids, however, deterred the Chileans from landing troops on the coast of the Bolivian littoral. Effectively, with the bulk of the Chilean fleet in Valparaiso, the *Huascár* and the *Unión* were masters of the sea until the end of September, when the Chilean ironclads were ready to return to the fray. In recognition of this, in September, Grau was promoted to the rank of contralmirante.

By then, Riveros had divided his Chilean fleet into two divisions. Tenente Latorre of *Magallanes* was promoted to capitán and given command of the *Almirante Cochrane*, which with her sister ship *Blanco Encalada* formed the 1st Division, while the slower corvettes and gunboats were grouped into a 2nd Division. The intention was to use the unarmoured ships to draw the *Huascár* into battle, where she could then be set upon by the two ironclads. On 30 September, the Chilean fleet finally steamed north again, and by 1 October the two ironclads arrived off Arica. Riveros had fitted the ironclads' steam launches with spar torpedoes, and he intended to use them to attack the *Huascár* at night as she lay at anchor. The Peruvian ironclad, though, was at sea, so Rivero withdrew to Antofagasta. *Huascár* and *Unión* had cruised as far south as Coquimbo, a Chilean port between Antofagasta and Valparaiso. However, Grau returned north in *Huascár* when he discovered Rivero and his two Chilean ironclads were at sea.

On 23 July 1879, the Chilean steam transport *Rimac* was captured by the *Huascár* and *Unión* after being intercepted by them 18 miles off Antofagasta. She was finally taken following a four-hour chase south down the coast.

The battle of Angamos

Grau arrived off Antofagasta at 2.00am on 8 October, but Riveros' fleet wasn't there. He turned north, and at 3.00am smoke was spotted ahead of them. Three Chilean ships were sighted; Riveros' flagship *Blanco Encalada*, the gunboat *Covadonga* and the transport *Matias Cousiño* were heading south, down the coast. *Huascár* and *Unión* headed out to sea, then turned north towards the safety of Arica. However, at 7.15am Peruvian lookouts on *Huascár* sighted more smoke to the north-west. It was the *Almirante Cochrane*, the corvette *O'Higgins* and the armed transport *Loa*. With the rugged coast to starboard, Grau was now trapped between two enemy forces – one to the south and the other to the west.

He detached the *Unión* with orders to make for Arica. Despite a day-long pursuit by the *O'Higgins* and *Loa*, the Peruvian corvette managed to escape. The *Huascár*, though, would turn and fight. At 9.25am, *Huascár* opened fire on the *Almirante Cochrane* at a range of 3,000yds. Capitán Lattore, though, held his fire until the range had dropped to 2,000yds – a mile. His first salvo struck the *Huascár* and jammed her gun turret. As the range fell Grau tried to ram the *Cochrane*, but Lattore's more manoeuvrable ship managed to keep clear. The firing continued, with the range now less than 1,000yds. At 9.45am, a shell from the *Cochrane* struck the *Huascár's* conning tower, and Contralmirante Grau was killed. His crew though, were determined to fight on to the end.

By 10.10am, the *Blanco Encalada* had come within range of the *Huascár*, which was now off the headland of Punta Angamos, 30 miles north of where the action had first begun. By then the *Cochrane* and *Huascár* were circling each other at point-blank range, trading shots and attempting to ram each other, but without success. It was now clear though that the *Huascár* was being hit hard. Several Chilean shells had penetrated her armour, and at 10.20am a shell exploded inside the *Huascár's* turret, killing everyone inside. With that, she hauled down her colours, and a Chilean boarding party was sent across. They thwarted a last-minute attempt to scuttle the ironclad, which became a Chilean prize. The vicious little battle cost the lives of 32 of the

The inside of the armoured central battery of the Chilean ironclad *Almirante Cochrane*. One advantage of this design was the space available to work and train the guns. Pictured here is one of the six Armstrong 9in RMLs, with three mounted on each beam.

Peruvian crew, with another 48 being wounded. Chilean casualties amounted to just one dead and 11 wounded, all from the *Almirante Cochrane*.

The Chilean offensive

The loss of Contralmirante Grau was a grievous blow for the Peruvians, and their country was plunged into a period of national mourning. The loss of the *Huascár* – the country's last seagoing ironclad – ended any last hopes of victory. The *Huascár* was taken to Valparaiso for extensive repairs, and the following month she returned to sea under the Chilean flag, commanded by Capitán Manuel Thomson. The Peruvians now had no seagoing ironclads, while the Chileans had three. Effectively, this meant that control of the sea was securely in Chilean hands. They could now land troops virtually at will anywhere along the Peruvian and Bolivian coast, save for the well-defended ports of Callao and Arica. Contralmirante Riveros' strategy was therefore to impose a full blockade of these Peruvian ports, to destroy Peruvian infrastructure through coastal bombardment and raiding, and to support the army in any amphibious operations.

In August 1879, Contralmirante (Rear Admiral) Juan Williams Rebolledo was replaced as commander of the Chilean Navy by this man, Capitán Galvarino Riveros Cárdenas (1829–92), commander of the *Blanco Encalada*. His acting rank of contralmirante was confirmed after his victory at the battle of Angamos two months later.

A division of 10,000 Chilean troops under General Escala was gathered at Antofagasta and embarked on 15 transport ships. Various amphibious targets were suggested, but eventually the port of Pisagua in southern Peru was selected. At dawn on 2 November, the transports appeared off the port, escorted by Capitán Lattore in *Almirante Cochrane*, who also commanded the *O'Higgins*, *Magallanes* and *Covadonga*. Although the Peruvians had a sizeable force in the region, it was widely dispersed. Consequently, covered by a shore bombardment from Lattore's ships, the landing to the north of Pisagua was only lightly opposed. This was just as well, as the operation was badly muddled. Still, the town was taken that afternoon. After pausing for reinforcements, the Chileans moved inland, and although they were defeated at the battle of Tarapacá, the Peruvians were eventually forced to withdraw northwards towards Arica.

As a result, Iquique to the south was abandoned as the Peruvians pulled back. A landing party from *Almirante Cochrane* secured control of this key port three days later, on 23 November. This was an economic disaster for Peru, as it handed Chile control of the nitrate mines, the cornerstone of the Peruvian economy. A week earlier, Riveros in the *Blanco Encalada* had left Pisagua for a cruise up the Peruvian coast past Arica. Early on 18 November, he encountered the *Unión* off Mollendo, accompanied by the *Pilcomayo* and a transport. The Peruvians turned back towards Arica, but the *Pilcomayo* was hit and slowed, and eventually was captured. She was taken back to Valparaiso, from where she re-emerged as a Chilean warship.

The military setbacks led to unrest in Peru, and in late December Prado was forced from power after an armed uprising led by his political rival Nicolas Pierola. Once in office, though, President Pierola vowed to continue the war. A week later, President Daza of Bolivia was ousted in a coup, replaced by General Campero, but he was unable to gather enough support for a continuation of the war. Effectively then, Bolivia thus bowed out of the conflict, having already lost its Pacific littoral, and Peru was left to fight on alone. On 28 November, Rivero established a blockade of Arica, while sending other warships to blockade the smaller ports of Ilo and Mollendo to the north. Rivero also stationed his flagship *Blanco Encalada* above Arica, to intercept any Peruvian foray. This made it almost impossible for the Peruvians to supply their forces around Arica. The noose was then slowly tightened.

In late February 1880, landings were made at Ilo, and further inland the Peruvians were defeated, severing the land route between Lima and Arica. Simultaneously, on 27 February, Arica was bombarded by *Huascár* and *Magallanes*, prompting the Peruvian ironclad *Manco Cápac* to venture out to fight them, accompanied by a torpedo boat, the *Alianza*. The two ironclads pounded away at each other for two hours, but only one telling hit was scored, when a 15in shell from the Peruvian monitor struck the *Huascár*'s conning tower, killing Capitán Thomson – standing on the same spot where the ironclad's Peruvian captain had died. The battered *Huascár* withdrew, Thomson was replaced by the newly promoted Capitán Condell of the *Covadonga* and the blockade continued.

Other bombardments followed, but the *Manco Cápac* kept her distance. On land, the Chilean army expanded its bridgehead around Ilo, and on 26 May it defeated the Peruvian and Bolivian army at the battle of Tacna. This paved the way for an advance on Arica from the north, and by 5 June the port was invested. The key to its defence, a mountain on the southern side of the port, was stormed and captured two days later. Among those killed in the battle was Capitán Moore, who had run the *Independencia* aground the previous May. The port fell, and unable to escape, the *Manco Cápac* was scuttled to prevent her capture. The little torpedo boat *Alianza* tried to break through the blockade, almost evading its pursuers, but an overheating boiler ended the attempt and she was destroyed by her crew near Ite, 50 miles up the coast.

The fall of Arica meant that the key southern Peruvian provinces of Tarapacá and Tacna were now firmly in Chilean hands. Bolivia would take no further part in the war, so now the fighting would centre on the fight for the Peruvian capital of Lima and its fortified port of Callao, the last stronghold of what remained of the Peruvian Navy.

C

THE PERUVIAN IRONCLADS *INDEPENDENCIA* AND *MANCO CÁPAC*

1. The largest ironclad in the Peruvian fleet was the *Independencia*, an iron-hulled broadside ironclad, built in Britain during Peru's war with Spain in the mid-1860s. *Independencia* was protected by a similar 4½in armoured belt as the Peruvian turret ship *Huascár*. By the late 1870s though, this was no real match for the latest naval ordnance, including the 9in RMLs carried in the Chilean ironclads. *Independencia*'s main broadside battery consisted of a dozen Armstrong 70-pdr. (6.4in) RMLs, while on her upper deck she carried two more guns, a Vavasseur 250-pdr. (8in) RML forward, and a Parrot 150-pdr. (7in) RML aft. This then, gave a fairly potent armament, but these were never properly tested in battle, as *Independencia* ran aground and was wrecked during the Battle of Iquique in May 1879.

2. In the aftermath of the American CIvil War the Peruvian government bought two Canonicus class monitors from their builders in Ohio. These were renamed *Atahualpha* and *Manco Cápac*, rigged with masts and a breakwater, and then towed to Peru – a voyage that took 14 months. Like her sister, the *Manco Capác* was armed with a pair of Dahlgren 15in smoothbore shell guns, which fired a 350lb projectile. These were inaccurate and relatively short ranged, and took 15 minutes to reload, but given the right circumstances these were still potent weapons. *Manco Capác* fought the *Huascár* in February 1880, and was scuttled the following June, after the fall of Arica.

1

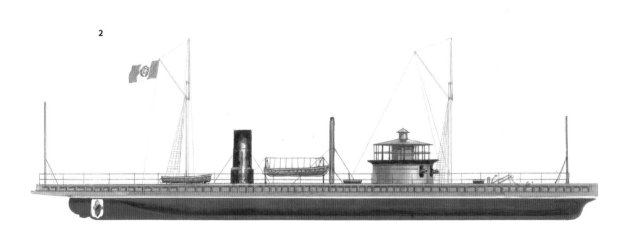

2

On 22 April 1880, after a deadline for neutral ships to leave the port, a Chilean squadron bombarded the Peruvian port of Callao. Pictured here, from the left, are the *Loa, Amazonas, O'Higgins, Angamos, Blanco Encalada, Huascár, Pilcomayo* and *Covadonga*.

On the night of 24/25 May 1880, while probing the defences of Callao harbour, two Chilean torpedo boats clashed with three Peruvian steam launches. During the fight, the torpedo boat *Janqueo* was blown up by the captain of the launch *Independencia*, who threw a charge on board and then detonated it with a pistol. Both vessels were wrecked by the explosion, with the loss of two Chilean and three Peruvian crewmen.

On 10 April, Riveros arrived off Callao and ordered all neutral ships to leave the port. The port itself was heavily defended by more than 30 large coastal guns and extensive fortifications. The Chileans bombarded the harbour on 22 April, but neither they nor the Peruvian coastal defences achieved anything. Still, the blockade had now officially begun, and would continue until the end of the year. Trapped inside the port were the monitor *Atahualpa*, the corvette *Unión* and several smaller warships. On the night of 25/26 May, the Chilean torpedo boats *Guacoldo* and *Janequeo* were patrolling off the harbour when, as they had four times before, they encountered three Peruvian steam launches; the *Independencia, Resguardia* and *Callao*. In this night-time clash though, crewmen on the *Independencia* threw an explosive charge aboard the *Janequeo*, and the ensuing explosion sank both craft.

It was a sign that the Peruvians were resorting to desperate measures. Sure enough, on 3 July, the Chilean armed transport *Loa* intercepted a small drifting boat filled with fruit and vegetables. The boat was booby-trapped though, and the charge detonated as the Chilean sailors brought her alongside. The explosion ripped a hole in the side of the *Loa*, which sank within minutes, claiming the lives of 118 of her crew. Six weeks later, it was the turn of the gunboat *Covadonga*. On 13 September, she came upon an abandoned sailing boat adrift off Chancay, 35 miles to the north of Callao. When she was brought alongside the *Covadonga*, a hidden charge exploded, sinking the gunboat with the loss of her captain and 72 of her crew. These booby-traps outraged the Chileans, who then in retaliation shelled Chancay, as well as the nearby ports of Ancón and Chorillos.

The blockade continued, but by early October Riveros had been reinforced by the *Huascár* and the *Angamos*. The ironclad had been refitted after her encounter with the *Manco Cápac*, and she now mounted a pair of experimental Armstrong 8in (20.3cm) 11.5 ton RBLs (rifled breech-loading guns), produced in Elswick in north-east England, which had a range of almost 8,000yds, or four sea miles. One of these was also carried on the *Angamos* on a revolving mounting. Until recently, the latter had been the *Belle of Cork*, a cattle ship, which had been bought by Chile as a troop transport and then converted into a gunboat. It first saw action off Arica, and was then sent to Callao, where it and the *Huascár* could bombard the port from 6,000yds, beyond the range of the coastal guns. Although no significant damage was done, this helped to demoralise the defenders. These guns were the forerunners of the Royal Navy's first modern breech-loading guns.

Early on 17 January 1881, as Chilean troops entered the Peruvian capital of Lima, the Peruvian Navy used explosives to destroy their fleet. Here, the corvette *Unión* is shown burning in the foreground, while in the port's dry dock an explosion rips apart the monitor *Atahualpa*. The remaining fires come from other unarmoured ships.

On 19 November the Chileans landed at Pisco, 200 miles south of Callao, and after reinforcing this bridgehead they began their advance on Lima. By late December, after another landing at Chilca, the Chileans had reached the main Peruvian defensive line south of Callao. In January the Peruvians were defeated at Chorillos and Miraflores, just south of Callao, and on 17 January the Chileans entered Lima. Late the previous evening the Peruvian Secretary of the Navy ordered the scuttling of the fleet trapped in Callao and the destruction of the port's coastal defences. So just before the Chilean troops entered the capital, the monitor *Atahualpa* and the corvette *Unión* were either set ablaze or destroyed with explosives. Five troop transports, the tiny submarine *Toro Submarino*, the torpedo boat *República* and the hulked steam frigate *Apurímac* were also destroyed.

It was the end for the Peruvian Navy. The following day, Lima's now defenceless port was surrendered to the victorious Chileans. The land war now became a long and hard-fought guerrilla campaign after the Peruvian troops withdrew northwards into the Andes. Other guerrillas established themselves in the mountains inland from Arica, near Lake Titicaca. The Chilean Navy supported the transport and supply of the army, but it was no longer actively involved in the fighting. In November 1883, they had a final chance to show their worth when they were asked to seize control of Lake Titicaca. So the torpedo boat *Colo Colo* was landed at Mollendo, hoisted onto a flatbed carriage, then moved by rail into the mountains. At the terminus of Polo, the ship was unloaded and floated on the lake.

There, 12,507ft above sea level, the *Colco Colo* became master of the lake. Peruvian communications

Having gained complete control of the sea, the Chileans were free to land troops wherever they wanted along the Peruvian coast. Here, transports land Chilean troops at Curuyacu, immediately to the south of Callao, before advancing to seize control of the port.

with Bolivia were quickly severed. This in turn encouraged the last of the Peruvian guerrillas there to surrender. It was a strange end to an equally unusual war. The naval campaign began conventionally, with a battle for control of the sea between two middle-range naval powers. It demonstrated the effectiveness of various types of warships and weapons, from central battery ironclads to long-range naval guns. It also saw, in its later stages, the introduction of torpedo boats and even a submarine, the attempted use of torpedoes and the successful deployment of shipborne booby-traps. In the end, though, the war ended with a clear demonstration of the effectiveness and importance of sea power.

THE CHILEAN FLEET

Of the two navies involved in the war, Chile's was the more professional, but due to government parsimony it lacked the maintenance facilities available to its rival. During the mid-1860s, both Chile and Peru had found themselves at war with Spain (a conflict known as the Chincha Islands War). It was the Spanish bombardment of Valparaiso in Chile and Callao in Peru in 1866 that spurred both countries to expand and modernize their navy. It was the Chileans though who, by 1879, had the more balanced fleet. In early 1879, the Chilean Navy had eight warships in commission, two more than its Peruvian counterpart. Of these, two were modern ironclads, the rest being steam-powered but unarmoured wooden-hulled warships – four corvettes and two smaller gunboats.

The ironclads *Almirante Cochrane* and *Blanco Encalada* were more modern and more potent than their Peruvian rivals, having been built in British shipyards following designs produced by Sir Edward Reed. He had been the Chief Constructor of the Royal Navy during much of the 1860s and was a proponent of the central battery ironclad – a marked improvement on the broadside ironclad design used for HMS *Warrior* (Britain's first armour-plated, iron-hulled warship commissioned in 1861) and the Peruvian ironclad *Independencia*. The real advantage of the central battery design was that protection was concentrated in an armoured box-shaped citadel which

Chilean warships at anchor off the navy's main base at Valparaiso, together with numerous merchant vessels. In the centre is the *Almirante Cochrane*, one of the two central battery ironclads in service with the Chilean navy at the start of the war.

enclosed the ship's gun battery. Essentially, it concentrated the armour in the place where it was needed most. While in theory this left other parts of the ship less well protected, Reed's design for his pair of Chilean ironclads also included a thick armoured belt running the length of the ship along the waterline, which reduced slightly at both ends.

Central battery ironclads: *Almirante Cochrane, Blanco Encalada*	
Builder	Earle's Shipbuilding Co, Hull, Yorkshire
Launched	January 1874
Commissioned	January 1875 (*Blanco Encalada* January 1876)
Displacement	1,800 tons (2,030 tons fully laden)
Dimensions	length overall: 210ft (64m); beam: 46ft 9in (14.2m); draught: 19ft 8in (6m)
Propulsion	two screws, powered by two Penn compound steam engines and six boilers, generating 2,960ihp (*Blanco Encalada* 3,000ihp); maximum speed: 12½ knots
Sail plan	two-masted barque rig
Armour	belt: 4½–9in(11.4–22.9cm) wrought iron with 12in (30.4cm) teak backing; battery: 6–8in(15.2–20.3cm) wrought iron with 12in (30.4cm) teak backing; conning tower: 4½in (11.4cm) wrought iron; deck: 2–3in (5.1–7.6cm) wrought iron
Armament	six Armstrong 9in (250-pdr) 12-ton RMLs in pivot mounts inside casemate, one Armstrong 20-pdr (4¾in) RBL and one Armstrong 9-pdr (3in) RBL on upper deck, and one Nordenfelt 1in machine gun in foremast top (*Blanco Encalada*: two Nordenfelts) Complement: 300
Fate	*Almirante Cochrane*: Rebuilt as a training ship in 1900, broken up in 1934; *Blanco Encalada*: Sunk in action by torpedo at Caldera Bay, Chile, on 23 April 1891

The central battery sat above the protective belt in the centre of the ship, and while slightly thinner than the belt, it was still more than adequate protection for the ordnance of the mid-to-late 1870s. Inside what amounted to an armoured citadel were six 9in rifled muzzle-loading guns, weighing 12 tons apiece, mounted on iron carriages and trained by means of rails set into the deck. Three of these large guns were mounted on each broadside. Amidships, the battery overhung the hull of the ship, with recesses fore and aft. This meant that these ironclads could fire three guns to each beam, while the two forward ones could also fire ahead and the two aftermost could fire astern. This gave the two Almirante Cochrane-class ironclads a virtually all-round arc of fire. With a muzzle velocity of 1,400ft per second, at close range their 250-pdr shells could smash through 11in of wrought-iron – more than adequate to penetrate the armour of the Peruvians' two seagoing ironclads.

Another advantage over their Peruvian counterparts was that the Almirante Cochrane-class ironclads had two propeller shafts apiece, each powered by a Penn compound horizontal trunk steam engine and three tube boilers. It was a modern propulsion system, and when first tested it gave the *Almirante Cochrane* a top speed of almost 13 knots. Officially, however, the maximum speed of the vessels was 12 knots. When the war began, both ironclads were slowed slightly by marine growth on the underside of their iron-built hulls. This reduced their speed by at least a knot or two. The year before, in 1878, the *Almirante Cochrane* had returned to Britain for refit and repair, so its hull was in better condition than that of her sister ship. To save wear and tear on the engines,

The Chilean fleet at sea. This engraving shows (from left to right in the port column) the fleet flagship *Blanco Encalada*, the corvette *Esmeralda* and the gunboats *Magallanes* and *Covadonga*. Behind them in the starboard column (also from left to right) is the second ironclad *Almirante Cochrane*, the corvette *Chabuco* (hidden behind the flagship), her sister ship *O'Higgins* and finally the corvette *Abtao*, between the *Esmeralda* and the *Magallanes*.

A Chilean squadron at their moorings in Valparaiso. In the foreground is the fleet flagship, *Blanco Encalada*, while moored off her port beam is the corvette *Abtao*, with her ochre funnel. The *Abtao* and the gunboat *Magallanes* briefly sparred with the *Huáscar* off Antofagasta in late August 1879.

they were also fitted with masts and sails, although there is little evidence these were used during the war.

During the War of the Pacific, the *Blanco Encalada* served as the flagship of the Chilean fleet. In terms of warship quality, she and her sister ship *Almirante Cochrane* enjoyed a demonstrable edge over their Peruvian opponents, which became increasingly clear as the naval campaign unfolded. They were sturdier ships, and any contemporary concerns about the fragility of iron hulls in action were proved unfounded. Tactically, they were easier to fight with than any of the four Peruvian ironclads, as their powerful broadside, faster reloading times and virtually all-round field of fire meant they could outperform their opponents in any gunnery action. Just as importantly, their hitherto untried 250-pdr cast-iron Palliser shells had been designed to penetrate an ironclad's armour. During the battle of Angamos in October 1879 they proved devastatingly effective.

The bulk of the fleet consisted of wooden-hulled steam-powered corvettes. These were small but powerful conventional warships, some of which were showing their age by the time the war began. The two largest were the sister ships *O'Higgins* and *Chacabuco*, both built in Britain just over a decade before during the Chincha Islands War. They had been interned until the armistice with Spain in 1868, and reached Valparaiso the following year. They carried a decent main armament of five Armstrong RMLs (rifled muzzle-loading guns), which made them the equal of the Peruvian corvette *Unión*. What let them down though, were their propulsion systems. By 1879, their boilers were in need of repair and their 14-year-old engines were considered inefficient. They could only make 9 knots, or probably a little less as the war progressed. Still, they were useful warships and were well-suited to the various tasks given them – the escort of troop convoys, the bombardment of shore positions and the blockade of enemy ports.

Steam corvettes: *O'Higgins, Chacabuco*	
Builder	R&H Green, Blackwall, London
Launched	1865 (*Chacabuco*, 1866)
Commissioned	1868
Displacement	1,101 tons
Dimensions	length overall: 216ft 6in (66m); beam: 33ft 4in (10.2m); draught: 18ft (5.5m)
Propulsion	single screw, powered by a Maudsley return connection rod steam engine and two boilers, generating 1,200ihp
Maximum speed	9 knots
Sail plan	three-masted barque rig
Armour	unarmoured
Armament	two Armstrong 7in (115-pdr) 7-ton RMLs on pivot mounts, two Armstrong 70-pdr (6⅜in) RMLs and four Armstrong 40-pdr (4¾in) RMLs, on broadside mounts, three guns on each beam
Complement	1,600
Fate	*O'Higgins*: decommissioned 1895, then used as a pontoon; broken up in 1905; *Chacabuco*: decommissioned 1890 and broken up

The fleet's two other steam corvettes were marginally less effective. The first had been built in Scotland for the Confederate Navy, which intended to use her as the commerce raider *Texas*. However, she was impounded, and in 1866 was bought by Chile, who renamed her the *Abtao*. The vessel was of composite construction, meaning the frame of the ship was wrought-iron, wood then being used to plank the hull. The *Abtao* was a three-masted barque-rigged vessel, with sleek lines and an elegant clipper bow, but she was also powered by a single propeller and steam engine, which at the time gave a top speed of 10 knots.

The *Abtao* had arrived in the Pacific too late to participate in the war with Spain, and she instead was used as a survey vessel. She remained in service until 1878, at which point she was decommissioned and sold. However, she was bought back into service early the following year, rearmed with a mixed battery of medium RMLs and smaller RBLs. The *Abtao* though was in poor shape, with a leaking hull and elderly engines that were now barely capable of making 6 knots. Still, she was used extensively during the war and subsequently underwent a major post-war refit in 1881.

The *Blanco Encalada*, flagship of the Chilean fleet during the war. Under Acting Contralmirante Riveros, she and her sister ship *Almirante Cochrane* were assigned to different divisions as part of his plan to lure the *Huascár* into battle and then trap her between the two Chilean ironclads. At the battle of Angamos, his plan worked perfectly.

Steam corvette: *Abtao*	
Builder	Denny Brothers, Dumbarton, Scotland
Launched	October 1863
Commissioned	June 1867
Displacement	1,600 tons
Dimensions	length overall: 211ft 6in (64.47m); beam: 42ft (12.7m); draught: 8ft (2.4m)
Propulsion	single screw, powered by a Maudsley return connection rod steam engine and two boilers, generating 800ihp
Maximum speed	10 knots
Sail plan	three-masted barque rig
Armour	unarmoured
Armament	three Armstrong 7in (115-pdr) 7-ton RMLs on pivot mounts, four Armstrong 40-pdr (4¾in) RMLs, two on each broadside
Complement	200
Fate	broken up in 1922

An even older vessel was the wooden-hulled steam corvette *Esmeralda*, which was over a quarter of a century old by 1879, having been laid down in Britain in 1854. She was commissioned into the Chilean Navy the following year, and saw service during the Chincha Islands War. *Esmeralda* was later used as a training ship, but was pressed into service as a front-line warship in March 1879. Like the other Chilean corvettes, she carried a three-masted barque rig to augment her steam engine. She had been extensively renovated a few years before, but she was still old and under-powered. The *Esmeralda*

The sleek Chilean corvette *Abtao*, pictured lying at her moorings off Valparaiso. Early on 28 August 1879, while anchored off Antofagasta, the *Huascár* launched a self-propelled Lay torpedo at the *Abtao*. However, the torpedo malfunctioned and turned back towards the ironclad. Disaster was only averted when an officer dived into the water to fend off the rogue torpedo.

was widely regarded as the slowest warship in the fleet, capable of making no more than 6 knots. She was sunk by the *Huascár* during the battle of Iquique in May 1879.

Steam corvette: *Esmeralda*	
Builder	William Pitcher, Northfleet, Kent
Launched	June 1855
Commissioned	September 1855
Displacement	855 tons
Dimensions	length overall: 210ft (64m); beam: 32ft (9.8m); draught: 14ft 2in (2.4m)
Propulsion	single screw, powered by two horizontal condensing steam engines and four boilers, generating 200ihp.
Maximum speed	8 knots
Sail plan	three-masted barque rig
Armour	unarmoured
Armament	fourteen Armstrong 40-pdr (4¾in) RMLs, seven on each broadside
Complement	200
Fate	sunk in action off Iquique on 21 May 1879

As well as the four corvettes, the Chilean Navy also had two gunboats. The most modern of these was the composite-built *Magallanes*, laid down on the Thames in 1872 and completed two years later. She had two propeller shafts, which made her manoeuvrable, and in theory she could make 11 knots, although 10 knots was probably closer to the mark. Her main armament of two Armstrong RMLs gave the *Magallanes* a reasonable punch, although before the war she was primarily employed as a hydrographic vessel rather than a front-line warship. Nevertheless, *Magellanes* proved a useful member of the wartime fleet.

Steam gunboat: *Magallanes*	
Builder	W&H Green, Blackwall, London
Launched	July 1873
Commissioned	December 1874
Displacement	950 tons
Dimensions	length overall: 200ft (61m); beam: 27ft (8.2m); draught: 11ft 6in (3.5m)
Propulsion	single screw, powered by a compound steam engine and two boilers, generating 2,230ihp
Maximum speed	11½ knots
Sail plan	three-masted barque rig
Armour	unarmoured
Armament	one Armstrong 7in (115-pdr) 7-ton RML, one Armstrong 64-pdr (6⅓in) 64cwt RML and one Armstrong 20-pdr (4¾in) RBL, all on pivot mounts
Complement	138
Fate	decommissioned in 1906, and sank off Corall, Chile, in 1907

The second gunboat was the *Covadonga*, a wooden-hulled Spanish vessel built in Cadiz for the Spanish Navy and commissioned in 1859 as the *Virgen de Covadonga*. This sleek, schooner-rigged vessel was designed as an *aviso* (despatch vessel), but during the Chincha Islands War she was used as a Spanish scouting vessel. *Covadonga* was captured by the Chilean corvette *Esmeralda* in November 1865, and the following month she was re-commissioned as the Chilean warship *Covadonga*. She had been modified slightly during the years, but by 1879 she was considered an elderly warship of limited combat value. The ageing Spanish engine could only give her a top speed of 7 knots. However, thanks to skilful handling by the ship's commander, the *Covadonga* proved her worth at the battle of Iquique, when she lured the Peruvian ironclad *Independencia* onto the rocks. The *Covadonga* was sunk in October 1880 by an explosive device hidden in a drifting boat.

Steam gunboat: *Covadonga*	
Builder	Arsenal de la Carrara, Cádiz, Spain
Launched	November 1859
Commissioned into Spanish Navy	October 1865
Captured by Chilean Navy	November 1865
Commissioned	December 1865
Displacement	630 tons
Dimensions	length overall: 159ft 1in (48.5m); beam: 23ft 4in (7.1m); draught: 11ft 10in (3.6m)
Propulsion	single screw, powered by a Ferrol compound steam engine and two boilers, generating 160 nominal ihp
Maximum speed	7 knots
Sail plan	three-masted schooner rig
Armour	unarmoured
Armament	two Armstrong 70pdr (6⅓in) RMLs and one Armstrong 12-pdr (3in) RML on pivot mounts
Complement	110
Fate	sunk by mine off Chancay, 13 September 1880

Another less significant Chilean warship at the start of the war was the small 240-ton paddlewheel steamer *Tolté*, built in France in the mid-1870s, and used as an aviso. During the war, other warships were added

The Chilean corvette *O'Higgins*, together with her sister ship *Chacabuco*, took part in the blockades of Iquique, Arica and Callao, and at the battle of Angamos the *O'Higgins* pursued the Peruvian corvette *Unión* while the Chilean ironclads took on the *Huascár*.

to the fleet, the most significant of which were the vessels captured from the Peruvians – the ironclad *Huascár*, the gunboat *Pilcomayo* and the torpedo boat *Alay*. The first two were repaired and commissioned into Chilean service under their old names, while the *Alay* duly became the Chilean torpedo boat *Guacolda* (i), which foundered off the Chincha Islands in April 1881.

When the war began, the fleet was augmented by a number of vessels purchased by the Chilean government. These included the Clyde-built merchant steamers *Loa* and *Amazonas*, which were used as patrol vessels. The 1,650-ton, five-year-old *Loa* mounted a pair of Armstrong 80-pdr (6in) RBLs, while the brand-new 2,000-ton *Amazonas* carried one single 80-pdr aft. Both were capable of making 12 knots. The *Loa* was sunk off Callao in July 1880. The three-year-old 1,180-ton *Belle of Cork* was also a Clyde-built ship, which after being used to transport a torpedo boat from London was renamed the *Angamos* and fitted with an Armstrong Elswick 8in breech-loading gun on a revolving plate, as well as a small 3in RBL. *Angamos* could make just over 14 knots, but spent much of the naval campaign on blockade duty off Arica and Callao, where her long-range gun was used to bombard shore targets. In addition, the Chileans purchased – or more usually chartered – a small fleet of 20 merchant steamers to use as troop transports, as well as more than a dozen coastal sailing vessels used to transport supplies.

When the war began, Chile ordered a flotilla of 13 assorted torpedo boats from the Yarrow & Company shipyard in Poplar, London. In October 1879, the first of these, the *Vedette*, arrived as deck cargo on the *Belle of Cork*, the future auxiliary warship *Angamos*. The rest were transported to Valparaiso as they were built. They varied in size, the tiny 5-ton *Colo Colo* and *Tucapel* and the 10-ton *Vedette* being dwarfed by the 30-ton *Janequeo* (i), which arrived before the end of the year. They were followed by 25-ton Fresia-class vessels (*Fresia*, *Lauca* and *Quidorna*) and 35-ton Glaura-class boats

D **THE CHILEAN STEAM-POWERED WARSHIPS *ESMERALDA* AND *COVADONGA***

1. The bulk of the Chilean navy was made up of wooden-hulled corvettes and gunboats – no real match for any of the Chilean ironclads. Of the four corvettes in the fleet the oldest and slowest was the *Esmeralda*, commanded by Capitán Arturo Prat. By 1879 *Esmeralda* was almost a quarter of a century old, and relatively small and lightly armed, compared to her three consorts. She was also one of the slowest warships in the fleet, her old, worn engines barely capable of making 8 knots. Still, *Esmeralda* remained a useful enough asset, and took part in the blockade of Iquique. It was there, in May 1879, where she was attacked by the Peruvian ironclad *Huascár*. Prat died a hero's death while attempting to board the ironclad, and the *Esmeralda* was sunk, after being rammed by the *Huascár*.

2. The fleet also contained two workmanlike gunboats, the *Magellanes* and the *Covadonga*, a prize from Chile's war with Spain a decade before. The *Covadonga* was used to blockade Iquique, and during the battle there, in May 1879, was pursued by the Peruvian ironclad *Independencia*. Teniente Condell though, commanding the gunboat, kept close inshore as he ran south, and off Punta Grusea, eight miles south of the port, he led the Peruvian ironclad onto the rocks. The *Covadonga* went on to play an important role in the war, until her destruction by a booby-trapped abandoned boat eleven months later.

1

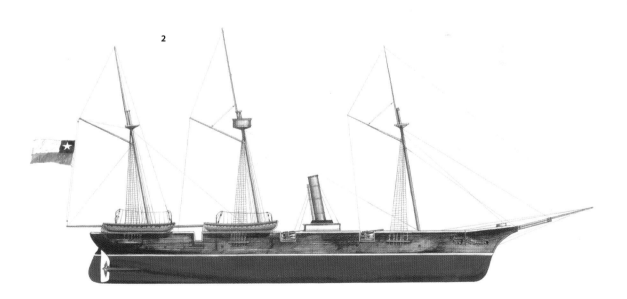

2

The gun deck of the Chilean corvette *Esmeralda*, pictured shortly before the war began. She carried 14 Armstrong 40-pdr rifled muzzle-loading guns (RMLs), seven guns to each broadside.

(*Glaure*, *Guacolda* (ii), *Guale*, *Janequeo* (ii), *Rucamilla* and *Tegualda*). The original *Janequeo* was sunk off Callao in May 1880, while the *Guacolda* foundered the following year. Newly arrived torpedo boats were given the names of these lost vessels. All of these craft were designed to use spar torpedoes – explosive devices on long poles protruding from the bows of the vessel. However, for the most part they were used as patrol boats or harbour defence craft.

The Chilean Navy had a number of advantages over its opponent. For the most part, its sailors were better-trained than their Peruvian counterparts; before the war, an emphasis was given to training in specialisms such as gunnery and marine propulsion, as well as seamanship. Generally, their level of education was better, as most hailed from around Valparaiso and had been adequately schooled, while the majority of Peruvian sailors had little or no education before joining the navy. This meant it was easier to school Chilean crews in complex mechanical tasks than it was for their opponents. Thanks to this peacetime training in gunnery, the accuracy and efficiency of Chilean crews was markedly superior to that of their rivals.

Naval officers were well trained too, most having attended Chile's own naval academy in Valparaiso. Before the war, many had been seconded to Royal Naval vessels, and so had gained a greater expertise in the operation of warships. This meant that senior officers generally had a better grasp of naval operations than their Peruvian counterparts. Where the navy fell down was in the maintenance of their vessels.

The Chilean Navy's main base at Valparaiso was poorly provided for in terms of repair or maintenance facilities, with no dry dock and little in the way of engineering or repair facilities. It did, however, have two small floating dry docks, suitable for the repair of vessels displacing less than a thousand tons. To some extent, the Chileans could also draw on commercial industrial facilities, such as the Valparaiso maintenance and repair workshops of the Pacific Steam Navigation Company. Without a dry dock, a task as commonplace as cleaning marine growth from a warship's hull became a major undertaking, involving laborious and difficult work by divers.

This situation improved as the war progressed, as equipment and expertise were purchased abroad. Generally, though, the Chileans remained poorly served in this area compared to the Peruvians, whose naval base at Callao was well equipped. This was exacerbated by geography: Valparaiso was 760 nautical miles from Antofagasta, 860 miles from Arica and 1,300 miles from Callao. Maintaining a naval blockade of these ports thus placed a strain on both ships and men. Forward supply and repair facilities were eventually established at Antofagasta, which served as a forward base for much of the campaign.

THE PERUVIAN FLEET

When the war began, Peru only had six serviceable warships at its disposal. Four of these, though, were ironclads. That said, only two of them were fully seagoing, and by 1879 the designs of both of these British-built warships were showing their age. The most modern of them was the *Huascár*, an iron-hulled turret ship of 1,800 tons. The term 'turret ship' was used to differentiate seagoing monitors from the coastal type developed by the US Navy during the American Civil War. *Husacár* had been built in Birkenhead, arriving in Callao in 1866 during the closing stages of the Chincha Islands War. Although she missed the action, when the warship reached Callao she was accompanied by a handful of Spanish merchant vessels captured during the voyage from Britain to Peru.

Her twin 10in RML guns provided a potent degree of firepower, and *Huascár* had an effective propulsion system, but the ship was let down by her armour. While this might have withstood the shot and shell of a decade before, by 1879 the *Huascár*'s armoured plates were arguably too thin to provide adequate protection from the large-calibre naval guns which were then entering service. Another flaw was that the vessel's turret had to be turned by hand, and it took 15 minutes to make a complete rotation. In action, it was probably easier to turn the ship than the turret. This made it difficult to aim and fire the gun accurately during a fast-paced close-range naval action. In fact, by the time the war began, *Huascár* had already undergone her baptism of fire.

Capitán Miguel Grau Seminario (1834–79) commanded the Peruvian ironclad *Huascár* during the campaign, and after a string of successes was duly promoted to the rank of Contralmirante. Both friend and foe alike dubbed him *El Caballero de los Mares* ('Gentleman of the Seas'). He was killed aboard the *Huascár* during the battle of Angamos.

Ironclad turret ship: *Huascár*	
Builder	Laird Brothers, Birkenhead
Launched	October 1865
Commissioned	November 1866
Displacement	1,800 tons (2,030 tons fully laden)
Dimensions	length overall: 219ft 6in (66.9m); beam: 35ft 9in (10.9m); draught: 18ft 8in (5.7m)
Propulsion	single screw, powered by a horizontal return connecting-rod steam engine and four boilers, generating 1,650ihp
Maximum speed	11 knots
Armour	belt: 2½–4½in(6.4–11.4cm) wrought iron with 13in (33cm) teak backing; turret: 5½–7½in(14–19.1cm) wrought iron with 11–13in (27.9–33cm) teak backing; conning tower: 2–3in (5.1–7.6cm) wrought iron; deck: 2in (5.1cm) wrought iron
Armament	two Armstrong 300-pdr (10in) 12.5-ton RMLs in a single twin Coles turret amidships, two Armstrong 40pdr (4¾in) RMLs on each beam, one Armstrong 12-pdr (3in) RML aft and one .44-cal Gatling machine gun in mainmast top Fitted with armoured iron ram bow
Complement	170–220
Fate	captured at Punta Angamos on 8 October 1879; subsequently served in Chilean Navy and survives as an historic ship

The Peruvian gunboat *Pilcomayo* took part in several actions during the war, under the command of Capitán de la Guerra and then Capitán Ferreyros, who assumed command of her in June 1879. The ship was captured by the Chileans the following November.

In May 1877, while the turret ship was anchored off Callao, the crew mutinied during an attempted presidential coup. They sided with the presidential rival, Nicolás de Piérola, against President Prado, but after putting to sea they earned the enmity of the British, having forcibly boarded British merchantmen while off the port. Consequently, the British consul requested that Rear Admiral de Horsey, commander of the British Pacific Station, give chase in his flagship HMS *Shah*, a steam-powered frigate. The *Shah* tracked down the *Huascár* off the small Peruvian port of Pacocha, and on the afternoon of 29 May gave battle, accompanied by the steam-powered corvette HMS *Amethyst*.

The engagement lasted for almost three hours, and despite the two British warships being unarmoured, they had the best of the clash, their rifled guns hitting the *Huascár* no less than 40 times. Thanks to the Peruvian ship's armour, however, these failed to cause any real damage. The *Huascár* slipped away under cover of darkness, foiling de Horsey's attempt to attack using the new Whitehead self-propelled torpedo. Meanwhile, the coup failed, and *Huascár* surrendered to the Peruvian authorities two days later.

The second Peruvian ironclad was the *Independencia*, another British-built vessel, this time constructed along the lines of the ironclad frigate HMS *Warrior*, although much smaller. The *Independencia* had been rearmed shortly before the outbreak of war and now carried 16 large RMLs on her gun deck and upper deck, making *Independencia* the most powerful warship in the Peruvian fleet. Like *Huascár*, she was fitted with a ram – a legacy of the naval fashion of the time – but unlike the turret ship the ironclad was better-designed for ramming tactics, as her hull below the waterline was divided by three watertight bulkheads. However, again like *Huascár* she suffered from a relatively thin armoured belt – the iron plates were the same thickness as those fitted to the small turret ship. The *Independencia* was powerful enough, but if she was drawn into a duel with one of the Chilean ironclads it was likely that their 9in shells would penetrate her gun deck with relative ease. In the end, though, this was never put to the test.

Broadside ironclad: *Independencia*	
Builders	Samuda Brothers, Poplar, London
Launched	August 1865
Commissioned	December 1866
Displacement	3,600 tons
Dimensions	length between perpendiculars: 215ft (65.5m); beam: 44ft 9in (13.6m); draught: 21ft 6in (6.6m)
Propulsion	single screw, powered by a trunk steam engine and four boilers, generating 2,200ihp
Maximum speed	12 knots
Sail plan	three-masted barque rig
Armour	belt: 4½in(11.4cm) wrought iron with 13in (33cm) teak backing; battery: 4½in (11.4cm) wrought iron with 13in (33cm) teak backing; deck: 2in (5.1cm) wrought iron
Armament	one Vavasseur 250-pdr (9in) RML on pivot mount amidships, one Parrot 150-pdr (7in) RML on pivot mount aft, two Armstrong 150-pdr (7in) RMLs in bow, 12 Armstrong 70-pdr (6⅜in) RMLs on gun deck (six on each beam) and two .44-cal Gatling machine guns on upper deck aft
	Fitted with armoured iron ram bow.
Complement	250
Fate	wrecked during battle of Iquique, 21 May 1879, and subsequently destroyed

Finally, the Peruvians also had two American-built monitors of American Civil War vintage. The *Atahualpa* and *Manco Cápac* were originally the US Canonicus-class monitors *Catawba* and *Oneota*. These were decommissioned by the US navy in early 1868 and returned to their Cincinatti builders, who duly sold them to the Peruvians. Their purchase represented something of a bargain for the Peruvians, as they were ideally suited to the defence of the Peruvian coast, or more importantly the Chincha Islands from the Spanish ironclad *Numancia*. These though weren't seagoing ironclads like *Huascár* and *Independencia*. So, to help them survive the long voyage from the Gulf of Mexico to the Pacific, by way of Cape Horn, they'd been modified slightly, with two masts added to carry barque-rigged sails and a breakwater fitted on the vessels' fo'c'scle.

Ironclad monitors: *Atahualpa, Manco Cápac*	
Atahualpa	
Builder	Alexander Swift & Co, Cincinnati, Ohio
Launched	April 1864 as USS *Catawba*, a Canonicus-class monitor
Sold to Peru	April 1868
Commissioned as *Atahualpa*	June 1870
Manco Cápac	
Builder	Alexander Swift & Co, Cincinnati, Ohio
Launched	May 1864 as USS *Oneota*, a Canonicus-class monitor
Sold to Peru	April 1868
Commissioned as	*Manco Cápac*: June 1870
Specifications	
Displacement	2,100 tons
Dimensions	length overall: 225ft (68.6m); beam: 43ft 3in (13.2m); draught: 13ft 6in (4.1m)
Propulsion	single screw, powered by a vibrating-lever steam engine and two boilers, generating 320ihp
Maximum speed	8 knots (reduced to 6 knots by 1879)
Sail plan	two-masted barque rig added in 1868
Armour	belt: 5in (12.7cm) wrought iron; gun turret: 10in(25.4cm) wrought iron; conning tower: 10in (25.4cm) wrought iron; deck: 1½in (3.8cm) wrought iron
Armament	two Dahlgren 15in (450-pdr) smoothbores in single twin Ericsson turret
Complement	100
Fate	*Atahualpa*: Scuttled in Callao, 17 January 1881; *Manco Cápac*: Scuttled in Arica, 7 June 1880

They reached Callao after a 14-month voyage, and were duly commissioned into the Peruvian Navy, with *Atahualpa* serving as a port guardship at Callao and *Manco Cápac* at Arica. Their lack of general seaworthiness though and their slow speed meant they were unfit for any more active form of service. When the war began, both ships were in Callao, but the *Manco Cápac* was subsequently escorted to Arica before the Chileans imposed their blockade of the port. Although their American-manufactured Dahlgren 15in smoothbore guns were considered obsolete, they had a hefty degree of striking power, which compensated somewhat for their lack of either range or accuracy. During the subsequent engagement between the *Manco Cápac* and the ironclad *Huascár*, by then in Chilean hands, the brute force of the monitor's firepower was plainly evident.

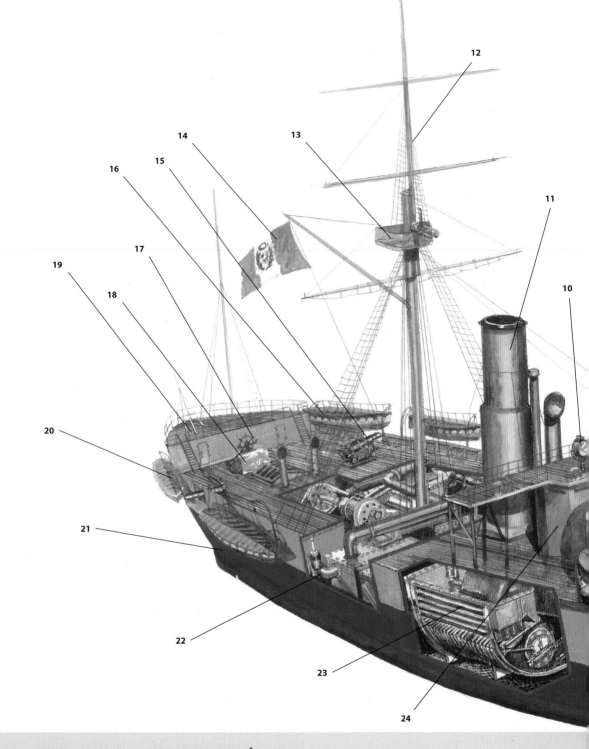

12

14

13

15

16

11

17

19

18

10

20

21

22

23

24

E

THE PERUVIAN IRONCLAD *HUASCÁR*, 1879

The flagship of the Peruvian navy, the small iron-hulled turret ship *Huascár* had a chequered career, first seeing action during a Peruvian coup in 1877, when she fought two British warships. Two years later, during the War of the Pacific, *Huascár* sank the *Esmeralda* at the Battle of Iquique in May 1879, then raided her way along the coast of Chile and the Bolivian littoral. As a result her commander, Capitán Miguel Grau was promoted to the rank of Contralmirane. For a while Grau and *Huascár* seemed unstoppable. Then though, in October, the *Huascár* sailed into an ambush off Antofagasta, sprung by the Chilean ironclads *Almirante Cochrane* and *Blanco Encalada*. In the ensuing Battle of Angamos *Huascár* was battered into submission and captured, while Grau was killed at his post in his flagship's conning tower.

KEY

1 Iron ram
2 Raised forecastle
3 Anchor cables
4 Capstan
5 Access to crew quarters
6 Position of foremast (removed before outbreak of war)
7 Cole turret
8 Armstrong 10" RML (one of two)
9 Armoured conning tower
10 Flying bridge
11 Retractable funnel
12 Mainmast
13 Fighting top, containing Gatling machine gun
14 Peruvian ensign
15 Armstrong 40-pdr. RML (one of two)
16 Ship's boat (one of four)
17 Emergency wheel
18 Access to wardroom
19 Poop deck, with Armstrong 12-pdr. RBL inside, mounted as a stern chaser
20 Captain's gig on starboard quarter stern davits
21 Rudder, and single propeller
22 Engine room
23 Boiler room
24 Wheelhouse (beneath conning tower)
25 Main magazine
26 Armoured belt (4 ½in thick)

Ironclad turret ship: *Huascár*

Builder	Laird Brothers, Birkenhead
Launched	October 1865 Commissioned: November 1866
Displacement	1,800 tons
Dimensions	length overall: 219ft 6in (66.9m) Beam: 35ft 9in (10.9m) Draught: 18ft 8in (5.7m)
Propulsion	single screw, powered by a horizontal return connecting-rod steam engine and four boilers, generating 1,650 ihp. Maximum speed: 11 knots
Armour	belt: 2.5–4.5in (6.4–11.4cm) wrought-iron with 13in (33cm) teak backing. Turret: 5.5–7.5in (14–19.1cm) wrought iron with 11–13in (27.9-33cm) teak backing. Conning tower: 2–3in (5.1–7.6cm) wrought-iron Deck: 2in (5.1cm) wrought-iron.
Armament	two Armstrong 300-pdr. (10in) 12.5 ton RMLs in a single twin Coles turret amidships, two Armstrong 40pdr. (4.7in) RMLs on each beam, one Armstrong 12-pdr. (3in) RML aft. and one 0.44in Gatling machine gun in mainmast top Fitted with armoured iron ram bow
Complement	170–220

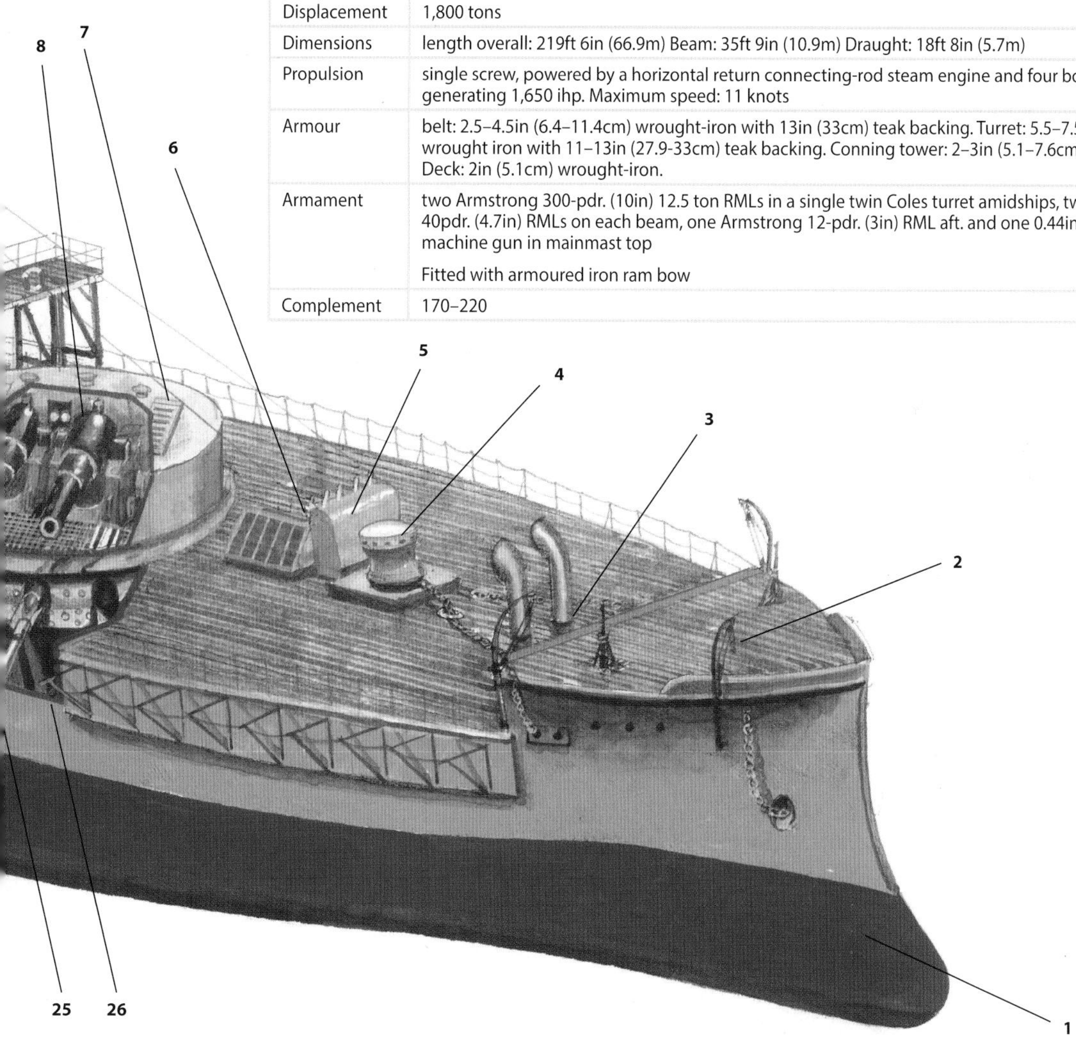

In addition to its four ironclads, the Peruvian fleet included a number of wooden-hulled steam-powered vessels of various sizes. Only two of these were of any use as warships, the remainder serving as armed steamers or makeshift transports of little military value. The larger of these two unarmoured warships was the *Unión*, a wooden corvette of 1,500 tons built in France in 1864–65 for the Confederate Navy as the *Shanghai*, to be renamed the *Georgia* when commissioned. She never entered service, due to an embargo, and instead was sold to Peru while still under construction, together with her sister ship *San Francisco* (which would have become the Confederate raider *Texas*). The latter became the Peruvian corvette *America*, but she was destroyed by a tidal wave in 1868, so by 1879 only the *Unión* remained in service. Although now elderly, her engines and boilers had been overhauled shortly before the outbreak of war, and *Unión* was fully seaworthy. She carried a fairly impressive armament of 14 RMLs of various sizes, either mounted on upper-deck pivots or as broadside weapons on the gun deck.

Steam corvette: *Unión*	
Builder	Chantiers Dubignon, Nantes, France
Sold to Peru while under construction	November 1864
Launched	January 1865
Displacement	1,984 tons (2,016 fully laden)
Dimensions	length overall: 243ft (74.07m); beam: 36ft 5in (11.12m); draught: 17ft 5in (5.34m)
Propulsion	single screw, powered by a horizontal reciprocating steam engine and two boilers, generating 400ihp
Maximum speed	12 knots
Sail plan	two-masted barque rig
Armour	unarmoured
Armament	two Parrot 100-pdr (6⅜in) RMLs on upper-deck pivot mounts, 12 Voruz-Blakely 70-pdr (6⅜in) RMLs on gun deck (six on each broadside) and one Parrot 30-pdr (4⅛in) RML carried as boat gun
Complement	134
Fate	scuttled off Callao, January 1881

The remaining Peruvian warship of any note was the *Pilcomayo*, a wooden-hulled gunboat of 600 tons. She had been built in Blackwall on the River Thames four years before. Strangely, it was intended to call her the *Putamayo*, after a Peruvian river, but an error by the shipyard resulted in the gunboat being given the wrong name, which actually belonged to a river in

The Peruvian monitor *Atahualpha*, formerly the USS *Catawba*, a Canonicus-class monitor built during the American Civil War. After being sold to Peru, and before the long journey to Callao, she was fitted with masts and spars, plus an iron breakwater forward of the turret.

Bolivia and Paraguay. Rather than change it, the Peruvians kept the existing name. She carried a reasonably decent armament of four rifled guns, but was of limited fighting potential.

Steam gunboat: *Pilcomayo*	
Builder	Wigram & Sons, Blackwall, London
Launched	1874
Commissioned	March 1875
Displacement	610 tons (800 tons fully laden)
Dimensions	length overall: 171ft (52.12m); beam: 27ft 5in (8.35m); draught: 11ft (3.35m)
Propulsion	single retractable screw, powered by a Penn horizontal reciprocating steam engine and two boilers, generating 180ihp
Maximum speed	11½ knots
Sail plan	three-masted barque rig
Armour	unarmoured
Armament	two Armstrong 70-pdr (6⅖in) RMLs (one on each broadside), four Armstrong 40-pdr (4¾in) RBLs (two on each broadside) and one .44cal Gatling machine gun on fo'c'scle
Complement	130
Fate	captured at Tocopilla, 18 November 1879; susequently used as a Chilean hydrographic vessel until 1909

These six warships were the only effective ones in Peruvian service. However, when the war began there were others too. The 14-year-old patrol vessels *Limeña* (1,163 tons) and the six-year-old *Oroya* (1,600 tons) were both paddlewheel vessels, and so were largely unsuited to modern naval use due to their vulnerability to enemy fire. The Peruvians also had a small steam aviso of 310 tons called the *Talisman* and a 16-year-old steam transport ship of 990 tons called the *Chalaco*. These were all armed with an assortment of small guns; a pair of 6½in RMLs on the paddle steamers and four 3in or 4in RMLs on the others. They were of little use as warships, other than as scouting vessels, and so during hostilities all four of them were used as transports. In January 1881, they were all destroyed in Callao to prevent their capture, together with the 1,800-ton steam transport *Rimac*, which had been captured from the Chileans a year-and-a-half before.

Shortly before the war began, the Peruvian government bought three modern torpedo boats from the United States. Two of these, the *Republica* and *Alianza*, had been delivered before the outbreak of hostilities, after being shipped to Panama in crates and then assembled on the Pacific coast. They were both built by the newly formed Herreshoff Manufacturing Company of Bristol, Rhode Island. The Herreshoff brothers had designed a small experimental torpedo boat for the US Navy, and the Peruvians decided they wanted their own version. These small boats were capable of making 16 knots and could carry a pair of spar torpedoes. Both of these US-built small craft played a reasonably active part in the naval war.

Some confusion surrounds the *Alay*, a third Peruvian torpedo boat. It has been claimed she was the third of the Herreshoff boats, but she was also it was alleged a

The Peruvian steam gunboat *Pilcomayo*, pictured in Valparaiso undergoing repairs after her capture by the Chilean ironclad *Blanco Encalada* off Mollendo in November 1879. Her crew attempted to scuttle the vessel, but were prevented from sinking the gunboat by a Chilean boarding party.

larger vessel, built in Chester, Pennsylvania. Whatever the case, she was assembled in Panama and then crewed by the Peruvians. However, upon reaching Ballenita in Ecuador, the *Alay* was captured by a Chilean armed transport, which towed the vessel to Valparaiso. She was subsequently commissioned into the Chilean Navy as the *Guacolda*. In addition, during the blockade of Callao, the Peruvians gathered together five local steam launches and small steam tugs – the *Arno*, *Capitani*, *Indepedencia*, *Resguardia* and *Urcos* – which were used as lightly armed harbour patrol craft.

The principal base of the Peruvian Navy was Callao, the harbour of Lima. It was a secure harbour, being well-protected by coastal defence batteries, although many of these guns were considered outdated by 1879. Still, the small fleet was reasonably well served by repair facilities, which included both a purpose-built dry dock and a modern floating dry dock. This meant that at the start of the war, Peruvian warships were for the most part in good condition – the two ironclads, for instance, had recently undergone a refit and were in excellent shape. It also meant that damage incurred during the war could be repaired in Callao. Secondary bases at Arica and Iquique, and to a lesser extent at Pisagua, were essentially commercial ports, with very limited naval facilities.

The Peruvian fleet, although small, was well provided for in terms of ships, and while its ironclads were not as modern as their Chilean counterparts, they could make a good showing of themselves if well handled.

One advantage the Peruvians enjoyed over their Chilean opponents was the repair facilities available to them in their main base in Callao. Here, the broadside ironclad *Independencia* is pictured inside the base's floating dry dock. A conventional dry dock was also available.

PERUVIAN STEAM-POWERED WARSHIPS *UNIÓN* AND *PILCOMAYO*

1. The largest conventional warship in the Chilean Navy, the *Unión* was built in France for the Confederate Navy, who planned to use her as a commerce raider called the *Georgia*. The vessels were embargoed though, before being completed, and the *Georgia* (built under the false name *Shanghai*) and sister ship *Texas* (or *San Francisco*) were bought by the Peruvians. Capitán Grau, the future Peruvian admiral, commanded the newly-commissioned *Unión* on the long voyage to Callao, in company with the second corvette, which had been renamed *América*. The *Unión* would go on to see action in the Chincha Islands War with Spain. In 1871 *Unión* returned to Britain for a refit, and to receive new ordnance, although at the start of the war in 1879, she still suffered from mechanical problems. *Unión* played an active part in the war, seeing action off the Bolivian littoral, and participating in the Battle of Angamos. She was eventually burned at the hands of her crew in January 1881, just before Callao fell to the Chileans.

2. The elegant Peruvian gunboat *Pilcomayo* was built in Britain, and completed in 1874. *Pilcomayo* arrived in Callao the following January, and two years later formed part of the squadron sent to recapture the *Huascár* when the ironclad sided with the rebels during an attempted revolt against the Peruvian government. At the start of the War of the Pacific she was commanded by Capitán de la Guerra, and served as the consort of the corvette *Unión*. The two Peruvian warships took part in the opening naval clash of the war – a skirmish with the Chilean gunboat *Magallanes*. Then, under the command of Capitán Ferreyros, the *Pilcomayo* operated off the Bolivian littoral, before being stationed at Arica. On 18 November 1879 though, *Pilcomayo* was overhauled by the Chilean ironclad *Blanco Encalada*, and after a brief fight Ferreyros tried to scuttle the gunboat. The Chileans though, boarded her, and kept her afloat. So, the *Pilcomayo* ended the war under the Chilean flag.

This, however, was the main problem with the fleet. Although a naval academy had been founded at Callao, and Peruvian officers for the most part were both dedicated and competent, they lacked extensive training in modern naval weapons and tactics. Most technical departments such as ordnance and marine engineering were left in the hands of foreign-born officers or Peruvian mariners brought in from the country's mercantile community. This meant that Peruvian commanders often lacked the specialist knowledge they needed to get the best out of their ship. Their crews also lacked anything other than the most basic of naval training. While competent enough seamen, their lack of training in gunnery became all too apparent once the fighting began in earnest.

THE IRONCLADS IN ACTION

The naval side of the War of the Pacific involved a surprising range of actions, from major engagements involving ironclads to nocturnal clashes between torpedo boats and harbour defence craft. As space here is limited, it might be most profitable to look at the clashes involving the ironclads. After all, that was the area which really decided the outcome of the naval war and was what most interested contemporary observers around the globe. Of these, the principal engagements were the battles of Iquique and Angamos. Also of interest is the clash between turret ship *Huascár*, by then in Chilean hands, and the Peruvian monitor *Manco Cápac* off Arica in February 1880. Looking at how these clashes unfolded may give us a better understanding of the effectiveness of these ironclads in action.

Iquique, 21 May 1879
Of the three maritime encounters, the battle of Iquique was the only one which didn't involve a clash of ironclads. Instead, it centred around a duel between the Peruvian turret ship *Huascár* and the unarmoured Chilean corvette *Esmeralda*. The battle began at 8.15am when the *Huascár* opened fire with her twin 10in RBLs, and ten minutes later a shell struck the *Esmeralda*'s starboard side but passed right through the wooden hull. The ship's surgeon and his assistant were killed, together with a sailor. Capitán Prat of the *Esmeralda* moved close inshore, and as the town was held by

On 29 May 1877, the Peruvian ironclad *Huascár*, then in rebel hands, was attacked by British warships, the steam frigate HMS *Shah* and steam corvette HMS *Amethyst*, off the port of Ilo in southern Peru. The engagement was indecisive, despite the British warships being unarmoured, thanks largely to the poor standard of Peruvian gunnery.

the Peruvians the *Huascár* was now at risk of firing on its own troops. By then, the two other warships involved – the Peruvian ironclad *Independencia* and the Chilean gunboat *Covadonga* – had moved off to the south, leaving Prat and Capitán Grau of the *Huascár* to continue their duel alone.

Grau was worried that the *Esmeralda* might be using torpedoes, so he stopped his ship 600yds away and resumed the gunnery duel just before 9.00am. Fire from the *Huascár* was both slow and inaccurate. Grau's guns took between ten and 12 minutes to reload, and even then, as the turret was trained manually – and the guns also – accuracy proved a real problem. Over the next hour, *Huascár* fired ten rounds, five from each gun, and none of her 300-pdr Palliser shells hit their target. The *Esmeralda* fired much more rapidly, but *Huascár*'s armour was proof against the corvette's 40-pdr shells, which kept bouncing off the ironclad's hull and turret. By 10.00am, fire from the shore had increased, a Peruvian battery firing at *Esmeralda* from 450yds away. So, Capitán Prat decided to get underway again, but was immediately faced by a boiler malfunction.

With the corvette's speed now reduced to just 2 knots, she limped further out of range from the battery on the shore. This move encouraged Grau to move closer, and the range dropped to around 150yds. At that range, even *Huascár*'s gunners couldn't miss. Sure enough, a shell hit *Esmeralda* squarely amidships, just above the waterline on the port side. It exploded in the corvette's engine room, killing many of those working there. A fire also started on the upper deck. It was now 8.30pm. Grau decided to ram the now-stationary Chilean ship, but the angle of attack was poor and the ironclad glanced down the corvette's port side. Amazingly, as the two ships lay alongside each other, Prat jumped aboard the enemy ironclad, accompanied by a petty officer, Sergeant de Dios. Both men were cut down by small-arms fire.

Meanwhile, Grau manoeuvred around for a second ramming attempt, which sprung leaks and caused flooding on the Chilean ship, but produced no immediate result. As the two ships clashed, Teniente Serrano jumped aboard the ironclad at the head of 12 men, but he and most of them were shot. The survivors jumped over the side. The *Esmeralda* was by then stationary in the water, flooding making her ride lower in the water. It was now almost noon. Grau backed off, turned in a circle and lined up the *Huascár* for a third ramming attempt. This time he struck the *Esmeralda* at a near-perfect right angle while making ten knots, the blow coming amidships on the corvette's starboard side. As the *Huascár* backed off, her crew could see they had been holed at the waterline and were

The Peruvian broadside ironclad *Independencia* was built in Britain during the 1860s, but by 1879 was showing her age, lacking the armoured protection of her Chilean adversaries. During the war, until her loss during the battle of Iquique, the ironclad was commanded by Capitán Moore.

The unarmoured Chilean sloop *Esmeralda* was slow, elderly and relatively lightly armed, but under the command of Capitán Prat she still put up a brave fight when attacked by the *Huascár* during the battle of Iquique.

A dramatic depiction of the final ramming of the unarmoured Chilean corvette *Esmeralda* at the battle of Iquique, during her one-sided fight with the Peruvian ironclad *Huascár*. The ironclad made three ramming attacks during the battle. Copy of an oil painting by Thomas Somerscales.

sinking. At 12.10am, the Chilean warship went down, leaving survivors and flotsam bobbing in the water. With that, *Huascár* edged in again to begin rescuing the men from the water.

Angamos, 8 October 1879

Upon encountering the Chilean ironclad *Blanco Encalada* and two other warships to the north of Antofagasta, Contralmirante Grau felt he could outrun them. So he manoeuvred his two ships *Huascár* and *Unión* to seaward of them. His aim was to escape northwards to Arica. Then, at 7.15am, the ironclad *Almirante Cochrane* and two other ships were sighted to the west. Grau was neatly caught between two forces. After detaching the *Unión* he altered course towards the *Encalada*, hoping to force his way past her and escape to the north before the two enemy squadrons could join forces. Grau was counting on the *Huascár*'s superior speed to avoid the rapidly closing trap. However, the *Almirante Cochrane*, commanded by Capitán Latorre was faster than Grau had expected, and was making 12 knots – a comparable speed to the *Huascár*. At 9.11am, when the range had dropped to 3,000yds, *Huascár* opened fire.

These shells missed, but surprisingly her second salvo scored a hit, the 300-pdr Palliser shell skipping off the surface of the sea to strike the ironclad aft. However, it didn't explode and damage was minimal. Then at 9.17am, when the range had dropped to 2,000yds, the *Almirante Cochrane* returned fire. Two of the three-shell broadside hit the *Huascár*, one striking the starboard fo'c'sle just forward of the turret, ripping a hole in the deck. Another

The *Manco Cápac*, formerly the USS *Oneota*, was completed too late to play a part in the American Civil War, and so in 1868 she was sold to Peru. During the War of the Pacific, she was stationed at Arica, and in February 1880 the vessel bested the ironclad *Huascár* in a duel.

shell penetrated the port side of the hull further aft, near the engine room. The explosion killed 12 crewmen. Then it was the turn of *Huascár*, which hit the Chilean ironclad with one of two 10in shells, but the huge projectile failed to penetrate the 6in armour plates protecting *Cochrane*'s central battery. This was a clear demonstration that the Peruvian ironclad had met her match.

So, Grau decided to change tactics. If he couldn't force his way past the Chilean using his guns, he would try ramming – a tactic that had served him well at Iquique. Both ships kept up a well-sustained fire, as Rivero on the *Blanco Encalada* approached from the north to support Lattore's ironclad. At around 9.40am, Grau began his manoeuvre, but the *Cochrane* sidestepped the *Huascár* and ended up on a parallel course, about 200yds off its beam. Minutes later, three Chilean 9in RMLs fired at the *Huascár*, and one of the shells struck the small conning tower, where Grau was standing. Its steel-plate armour didn't save him, and the tower was ripped apart by the explosion, and the Peruvian admiral and two of his men were eviscerated. This also damaged the ship's wheel in the steering compartment below the conning towers, and it took several minutes to restore control of the ship.

Then the Peruvian ironclad was hit again, this time on her turret. The shell penetrated its armour and exploded, killing or wounding everyone inside and partly damaging the starboard gun. Effectively, the *Huascár* was now out of action. Although one of the guns was still undamaged the ironclad was temporarily unable to defend herself as the two Chilean ironclads moved in for the kill. Capitán de Corbeta (Lieutenant Commander) Aguirre took charge, ordering his men to remove the mangled bodies and re-crew the blood-soaked guns. These men though, weren't trained gunners. Surprisingly then one of the last shots from *Huascár* struck the *Almirante Cochrane* in the stern, and Lattore temporarily turned away from the fight. By then, though, the *Blanco Encalada* had joined in and the battering continued.

By now it was 10.25am, and the action halted for a few minutes as the *Huascár*'s ensign was shot away. The Chileans ceased fire, thinking *Huascár* had finally struck her colours. However, when Teniente Palacios hoisted another ensign, the Chilean ironclads resumed firing and the first shell killed the courageous Palacios. Then, at around 10.30am, another shell from *Encalada* smashed into the turret again, killing more of its crew, including Lieutenant Commander Aguirre. The battered *Huascár* was now reduced to one damaged gun, and as the turret training mechanism was wrecked, it could only be aimed by turning the ship using the damaged steering gear. However, her Peruvian crew remained defiant, firing two more shots at the *Blanco Encalada* before a burst steam pipe ended their attempts to manoeuvre the ship.

By 10.50am, the last surviving officer, Teniente Garezon, decided to scuttle the wrecked ironclad, and ordered her sea cocks to be opened. Five minutes later the remaining crew began to abandon ship. Rivero ordered a boarding party to be sent over from the *Blanco Encalada*, and the Peruvian engineer was forced at pistol point to close the sea cock valves. The half-flooded and much-battered ironclad remained afloat, and eventually made

A depiction of the opening moments of the battle of Iquique on 21 May 1879. On the left, the Peruvian ironclad *Huascár* is pictured firing at the Chilean corvette *Esmeralda*, lying close to Iquique Island, while the *Esmeralda* has moved nearer inshore, close to the Peruvian-held port.

it to Mejillones, ten miles away, where *Huascár* was pumped dry. Of the ironclad's 194 Peruvian crew, 34 had been killed, 26 wounded and the remainder, demoralised and shell-shocked, were captured. Chilean losses, all from the *Cochrane*, amounted to one dead and nine wounded. Afterwards, the wrecked *Huascár* was repaired, and taken into Chilean service.

Arica, 27 February 1880

During the blockade of the Peruvian port of Arica, the Chilean blockading squadron was reinforced by the newly repaired *Huascár*, now flying Chilean colours. On the morning of 26 February, her new commander, Capitán Manuel Thomson, closed with the port and duelled with shore batteries. The ship was hit three times, but no real damage was done. The following morning Thomson steamed in again, this time to shell a train he saw heading north out of the town. This time, the *Huascár* was hit by a shell from a coastal gun, which penetrated her armour and caused some internal damage. It also killed seven men and wounded nine others. At that moment, the Peruvian ironclad *Manco Cápac* headed out from the shore to engage the *Huascár*, accompanied by the Peruvian torpedo boat *Alianza*, Thomson tried to keep his distance in case the *Alianza* attempted to attack him using its spar torpedo. However, the *Alianza* backed off, and the turret ship and the monitor cautiously approached each other.

Thomson tried to cut off the *Manco Cápac*'s retreat by placing his ship between it and the port. Capitán Lagomarsino of the *Manco Cápac* responded by heading straight for the *Huascár*. At 2pm, when the range had dropped to just 200yds, the lumbering Peruvian monitor opened fire with her two Dahlgren 15in smoothbores. In all, nine salvos were fired by the monitor during the 90-minute engagement. Despite the short range, almost all of the Peruvian shots missed. At around 3.15pm though, one of these enormous 450-pdr projectiles smashed into the *Huascár*'s conning tower. Thomson was killed instantly and his three assistants were gravely wounded.

It was a repeat of the tragedy which had befallen Contralmirante

A depiction of the Peruvian turret ship *Huascár*, as she looked after the battle of Angamos, fought on 8 October 1879. *Huascár* was hit by at least 20 Armstrong 9in shells during the battle, which wrecked her conning tower, knocked the turret out of action and peppered the funnel. Nevertheless, the battered ironclad remained afloat and was captured by her Chilean opponents.

A diagram showing the location of the hits inflicted on the *Huascár* during the battle of Angamos in October 1879. The truly debilitating shots were those that struck the ironclad's conning tower, killing Contralmirante Grau (labelled h), and those that penetrated the turret and killed or wounded the gun crews (a and b).

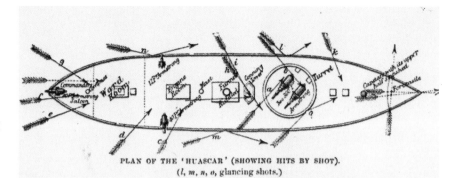

PLAN OF THE 'HUASCAR' (SHOWING HITS BY SHOT).
(*l, m, n, o,* glancing shots.)

Grau on the same spot just over four months earlier. The shot also brought down the *Huascár*'s foremast, which fell forward and jammed the turret, preventing it from turning. At 3.30pm, Thomson's deputy, Teniente Velvarde broke off the fight and headed back out to sea. The *Huascár* had lost eight men killed and 17 wounded, but the ironclad was quickly repaired off Antofagasta and re-joined the blockading squadron the following evening.

ANALYSIS AND CONCLUSION

These three actions underline several problems with the *Huascár*. First, her belt and turret armour offered insufficient protection against large modern ordnance fired at close range. In two of these three engagements, the small 'phone-box-like' conning tower behind the turret, protected by armoured plate just 3in thick, was little more than a death trap. One good hit could effectively put the ironclad out of action.

Off Punta Angamos, the *Huascár* was outgunned and outfought, both because the 9in Chilean guns had a slightly greater rate of fire inside their more commodious central battery and because their fire was more accurate. The latter was largely down to the gunnery skill of the crew, the result of more extensive training.

Then there was the vessel's capability to ram the enemy, a tactic used at the battle of Lissa in 1866, where the Austrians used rams to defeat their Italian opponents, and which dominated warship design and naval tactics for the next two decades. While the *Huascár*'s engines were powerful enough to

A depiction of the duel between two ironclads off Arica on 27 February 1880. The turret ship *Huascár* (left), now under Chilean command, was badly damaged by the Peruvian monitor *Manco Cápac* (right), and broke off the action. The Chilean commander, Capitán Thomson, was killed during the engagement.

drive her towards the enemy at speeds of up to 12 knots, the ship itself, with its single propeller wasn't sufficiently manoeuvrable unless its target, like the *Esmeralda*, was practically dead in the water. At Angamos, the twin-screwed Chilean ironclads were able to manoeuvre out of harm's way.

While the gun turret represented the future of naval gunnery, the Coles turret mounted in the *Huascár* was hand-operated, which meant it took too long to train against a target manoeuvring at close range. Off Arica, the *Huascár* fired 35 rounds, but these all missed the slow-moving *Manco Cápac*. While the monitor's obsolete Dahlgren 15in guns were inaccurate and the gun crews were inexperienced, they proved their value during the American Civil War, and at Arica in 1880 they showed that they still packed a punch.

This was still very much a period of transition in naval technology and tactics. So these three engagements involved everything from old monitors of the 1860s, armed with smoothbore guns, to modern ironclads just a few years old with effective rifled muzzleloaders. This was why, more than any real interest in the outcome of the war, the world paid such a keen interest to these events. For the global naval community, the real importance of the actions of Iquique, Angamos and Arica were the lessons they provided in the effectiveness of this largely untested naval technology.

FURTHER READING

Esposito, Gabriele, *The War of the Pacific*, Winged Hussar Publishing, Point Pleasant Beach, NJ (2018)

Farcau, Bruce W., *Ten Cents War: Chile, Peru & Bolivia in the War of the Pacific, 1879–1884*, Praeger, Westport, CT (2000)

Gardner, Robert (ed), *Conway's All the World's Fighting Ships, 1860–1905*, Conway Maritime Press, London (1979)

Gardiner, Robert (ed), *Steam, Steel and Shellfire: The Steam Warship, 1815–1905*, Conway Maritime Press (Conway's History of the Ship Series), London (1992)

Greene, Jack & Massignani, Alessandro, *Ironclads at War: The Origin and Development of the Armoured Warship, 1854–1891*, Combined Publishing, Coshohocken, PA (1998)

Hill, Richard, *War at Sea in the Ironclad Age*, Cassell, London (2000)

Hodges, Peter, *The Big Gun: Battleship Main Armament, 1860–1945*, Conway Maritime Press, London (1981)

De Lisle, Gerard, *The Royal Navy and the Peruvian–Chilean War, 1879–1881*, Pen & Sword Maritime, Barnsley (2007)

Olender, Piotr, *The Naval War of the Pacific 1879–1884: the Saltpeter War*, MMP Books (Maritime Series), Sandomierz, Poland (2020)

Padfield, Peter, *Guns at Sea*, Hugh Evelyn Ltd, London (1973)

Scheina, Robert L., *Latin America: A Naval History, 1810–1987*, Naval Institute Press, Annapolis, MD (1993)

Tucker, Spencer C., *Handbook of 19th Century Naval Warfare*, Sutton Publishing Ltd, Stroud, Gloucs (2000)

Warner, William E., *Warships of the Chincha Island War*, Amazon, Middletown, CT (2015)

Wilson, H. W., *Ironclads in Action: A Sketch of Naval Warfare, from 1855 to 1895* (Vol 1), Sampson Low, Marston & Co, London (1896)

INDEX